Dedication

For my family

Acknowledgments

I would first like to thank the editors and staff at Coaches Choice, and especially Kristi Huelsing, for making the book-producing process a pleasant one.

Special thanks to Judy Picone-Fadeyev, Creative Director of Davinci Corporation, for her skill and timeliness with the illustrations. Thanks to Charles Metzger, Strength and Conditioning Director of the New York Athletic Club, for his help with the conditioning section of the book.

And finally, thanks to all the hard-working softball players and coaches who make improvement a way of life. Good luck to all.

Peak Conditioning Training for Softball

Thomas Emma

©2005 Coaches Choice. All rights reserved. Printed in the United States.

No part of this book may be reproduced, stored in a retrieval system, or transmitted, in any form or by any means, electronic, mechanical, photocopying, recording, or otherwise, without the prior permission of Coaches Choice. Throughout this book, the masculine shall be deemed to include the feminine and vice versa.

ISBN: 978-1-58518-910-6
Library of Congress Control Number: 2004112087
Cover design: Jeanne Hamilton
Book layout: Jeanne Hamilton
Illustrations: Judy Picone-Fadeyev
Front cover photo: Todd Rosenberg/Allsport

Coaches Choice
P.O. Box 1828
Monterey, CA 93942
www.coacheschoice.com

Contents

Dedication 3
Acknowledgments 4
Preface 8

PART I: KEYS TO MAINTAINING PEAK PERFORMANCE

Chapter 1: Warm-Up, Cool-Down, and Flexibility 12
    Warm-Up
    Cool-Down
    Flexibility Training
    Pre-Movement Training Exercises

Chapter 2: Recuperation, Overtraining, Attitude, and Injuries 25
    Recuperation
    Sleep
    Overtraining
    Maintain a Positive Attitude
    Injury Prevention
    Injury Rehabilitation

Chapter 3: Softball Nutrition 35
    Components of Balanced Nutrition
    Weight Control
    Sample Meal Plans

PART II: SOFTBALL CONDITIONING

Chapter 4: Softball Conditioning Basics 46
    Energy Systems
    Physical Fitness for Softball
    Modes of Softball Conditioning

Chapter 5: Year-Round Softball Conditioning 53
    Aerobic Training
    Anaerobic Training
    Year-Round Conditioning Program for Softball

Chapter 6: Conditioning for Recreational Softball Players 60
          Program Parameters
          Conditioning Tips for Recreational Athletes

PART III: STRENGTH TRAINING FOR SOFTBALL

Chapter 7: Softball Strength Training Basics and Principles 68
          Why Strength Train for Softball
          Strength Training Basics
          Strength Training Principles
          Training the Core

Chapter 8: Core, Body Weight/Medicine Ball, and Upper Body Exercises 77
          Core Exercises
          Body Weight and Medicine Ball Exercises
          Upper Body Exercises

Chapter 9: Lower Body, Combination, and Softball Specific Exercises . .110
          Lower Body Exercises
          Combination Exercises
          Softball Forearm Series
          Softball Shoulder Series

Chapter 10: Year-Round Strength Training for Softball 133
          Year-Round Program
          Preparation Cycles (Cycles #1 and #2)
          Off-Season Cycles (Cycles #3-6)
          In-Season Cycle (Cycle #7)

PART IV: MOVEMENT TRAINING FOR SOFTBALL

Chapter 11: Balance Training 146
          Parameters of Balance Training
          Schedule Description
          Balance Exercises

Chapter 12: Speed Training 152
          Three Paths for Increasing Sprinting Speed
          Specialized Drills and Techniques for Enhancing Speed
          Speed Technique Drills
          Added Resistance Sprinting
          Overspeed Training

Chapter 13: Quickness and Agility Training 162
        Schedule Description
        Quickness/Agility Drills
        Quick Movement Drills
        Specific Movement Pattern Drills
        Random Movement Pattern Drills

Chapter 14: Plyometrics 169
        Developing Your Plyometric Program for Softball
        Schedule Description
        Keys to Safe and Productive Plyometric Training
        Beginner Plyometric Drills
        Intermediate Plyometric Drills
        Advanced Plyometric Drills

Chapter 15: Cross Training Options for Softball Players 184
        Play Other Sports
        Jumping Rope
        Stadium Step Running
        Spinning
        Boxing Training
        Sand Workouts
        Circuit Training

About the Author 190

Preface

The popularity of women's softball is bursting at the seams. At last count, nearly 350,000 girls were competing in high school softball and another 17,000 or so young women were playing collegiately. These figures are most likely conservative estimates, as more and more youngsters continue to pick up the game every year. And, if the numbers are not enough to convince you of softball's burgeoning popularity, how about the fact that the world's number one sports cable television station, ESPN, now carries the NCAA Women's Softball Playoffs on their network? Is there any doubt that softball has arrived?

With popularity, however, comes competition. And softball's unprecedented growth has led to fierce battles for roster spots, playing time, and team victories. In order to succeed in the current competitive climate, softball players must do everything humanly possible to improve. No longer is it enough to master the requisite softball skills of hitting, fielding, base running, pitching, and throwing. Players must come to the game in top-flight physical condition as well. Not doing so is a sure ticket to watching the action from the dugout or, worse yet, from an uncomfortable seat in the bleachers.

Conditioning yourself for softball is a year-round process that entails a variety of training disciplines including strength, flexibility, speed, balance, quickness and agility. Workout programs must be well planned, sport specific, and adhered to on a consistent basis. Additional components such as nutrition, individual recuperation requirements, injury prevention, and injury rehabilitation must also be taken into consideration by all softball players.

The book you're holding in your hands will provide the road map to softball conditioning success. It consists of four separate sections. Part I features strategies that will help you to maintain peak performance levels. The topics include warm-up, cool-down, flexibility, recuperation, sleep, overtraining, attitude, injury prevention and rehabilitation, along with an entire chapter on softball nutrition.

Part II deals exclusively with softball conditioning. It begins with the basics (energy systems and general softball fitness guidelines) and continues with explanations of aerobic and anaerobic conditioning. Also included are descriptions of a variety of training options from running to biking to swimming, along with a year-round conditioning schedule to help players and coaches with workout organization. The final chapter in Part II explains how the legions of recreational softball competitors can achieve peak physical conditioning levels.

Part III covers all aspects of strength training as it relates to softball. Over 60 different strength training movements, complete with exercise execution explanations and their corresponding illustrations, are featured in Chapters 9 and 10. A year-round strength-training program, which includes sample workout routines for each of seven training cycles, is detailed at the end of the section.

Part IV introduces you to movement training for softball. This section provides thorough descriptions of various techniques and drills that will help you to enhance your balance, speed, quickness, agility, and explosiveness. The final chapter in the book furnishes you with numerous cross training options that will make your training more interesting and more productive.

Fusing the training programs and information in *Peak Conditioning Training for Softball* with your energy, determination, and hard work will prove an unbeatable combination, one that will ensure that you reach your full potential on the softball field. Which, after all, is what it's all about.

A Special Note to Readers

The exercises and drills explained and illustrated in this book follow carefully planned guidelines. By using this information as presented, you will experience the best possible results. As with all exercise programs, be sure to see your physician before you begin.

PART I
KEYS TO MAINTAINING PEAK PERFORMANCE

1

Warm-Up, Cool-Down, and Flexibility

Without question, the two most neglected aspects of sports conditioning are the warm-up and cool-down. Unfortunately, many athletes, especially young athletes, complete with their indestructible attitudes, rush through or forsake altogether the warm-up process. Just as commonplace are athletes who forgo the post-workout cool-down, instead opting for the more pleasant experience of a warm shower and a bite to eat.

The temptation of bypassing warm-up and cool-down activities is certainly understandable. These disciplines are, in a word, boring. They are, however, also *essential* components of balanced conditioning, and all softball players, regardless of age or level, must take them seriously. The risks of not engaging in a thorough warm-up and cool-down are numerous and include falling short of your athletic potential and sustaining injury.

Warm-Up

Warming up prior to any type of intense physical activity, be it a game, conditioning workout, or practice, is a three-fold process. It includes *light exertion* for five to eight minutes, followed by a *comprehensive stretching* routine like the one detailed later in this chapter, and finishing with *low-intensity involvement* in the desired activity. Warming up correctly will contribute to productive workouts, enhanced performance on the softball field, and the prevention of injuries.

Cool-Down

The equally important cool-down process consists of a few minutes of *low-intensity activity* similar to the first step of the warm-up process, followed by an abbreviated *flexibility session* that focuses on stretching the lower back, hamstrings, and shoulders. Actively cooling down after high-intensity exertion of any kind will help the body recover, along with allowing it to return to its naturally relaxed state faster, thus promoting physiological balance and sound sleep. An example of the warm-up/cool-down continuum is detailed in Table 1-1.

Warm-Up Phase 1–Low-Intensity Activity
Perform five to eight minutes of light exercise, such as running in place, stationary biking, or slow-paced jogging. This type of activity raises your body temperature and gets the blood flowing to your muscles, which will allow you to stretch (phase 2) through a greater range of motion.

Prepares the body for

Warm-Up Phase 2–Flexibility Training
12 stretches (detailed in the next section)

Prepares the body for

Warm-Up Phase 3–Medium-Intensity Involvement in Desired Activity
Examples: Strength training—two light, high repetition (15 to 20) sets
Plyometric training—low-intensity bounding
Agility training—jumping rope at medium speed

Prepares the body for

Intense All-Out Activity

Cool-Down Phase 1–Low-Intensity Activity (See Warm-Up Phase 1)
Cool-Down Phase 2–Abbreviated Flexibility Routine
Six to eight stretches with an emphasis on the lower back, hamstrings, and shoulders.

Table 1-1. Warm-up/cool-down continuum

Flexibility Training

Flexibility training, while not as glamorous as strength training or plyometrics (detailed later in this book), is no less important. Every competitive (and non-competitive) athlete must make a priority of improving and maintaining flexibility. Regular stretching will make you less susceptible to injury, enhance recovery, and increase quickness, speed, and explosive power.

Flexibility work should be undertaken both before and after all competitions, practices, and conditioning workouts. Stretching prior to activity readies the body for strenuous exercise. Post-workout stretching aids in recovery, allowing lactic acid (lactate), a substance that contributes to muscle soreness, to be removed from the body efficiently. Less flexible athletes may want to include some extra stretching before breakfast in the morning and prior to retiring at night.

Because of the nature of their sport, flexibility training may be even more essential for softball players than for athletes in other sports. For example, unlike soccer players or basketball players, who basically remain in motion the entire time they're on the field or court, softball players experience considerable physical downtime during competition. This inactivity allows the body to cool and the muscles and joints to stiffen, therefore making athletes prone to pulled muscles and other related injuries. Stretching comprehensively and regularly on a year-round basis will take away some risk of injury.

Softball players should concern themselves with five types of stretching methods, including *static stretching, ballistic stretching, passive partner assisted stretching, proprioceptive neuromuscular facilitation (PNF), and rope/strap assisted stretching.*

Static Stretching

Static stretching will be the mainstay of a softball flexibility routine. It can be performed without assistance and entails slowly stretching a muscle to the point of slight discomfort but never to the point of pain. Each individual stretch should be held between 20 to 50 seconds. Static stretching, along with being extremely effective, is the safest of all stretching techniques.

Ballistic Stretching

Ballistic stretching uses dynamic, bouncing movements when stretching a muscle group. Many feel this abrupt contraction of the muscle is too dangerous, especially for young developing athletes. If an athlete chooses to incorporate this method, they should be sure that their muscles are sufficiently warmed up prior to stretching. Not doing so will leave them vulnerable to muscle pulls and tears. Ballistic stretching should not be used by injured athletes.

Passive Partner Assisted Stretching

Passive partner assisted stretching calls for having a partner add light pressure to each stretch to increase joint and muscle range of motion. For best results and to avoid injury, the partner should be experienced with this method along with having a good feel for the softball player's capabilities in terms of stretching.

Proprioceptive Neuromuscular Facilitation (PNF) Stretching

PNF stretching involves a partner/facilitator leading an athlete through a series of positions (contract, hold, relax, and movement) in 10-second intervals. In recent years, this technique has become very popular in the sports conditioning world and, if performed correctly and with the appropriate assisting personnel, can substantially increase muscle range of motion. Unfortunately, the majority of junior high and high school athletic departments, along with many smaller college programs, do not have individuals on staff who are experienced with PNF stretching. Incorrect execution of this method can lead to serious injury. Therefore, PNF stretching should never be incorporated unless the appropriate assisting personnel are on hand.

Rope/Strap Assisted Stretching

Rope/strap assisted stretching is similar to PNF stretching and passive partner assisted stretching in that it allows athletes to take their muscles through a greater range of motion. Unlike the two previously detailed stretching techniques, a partner/facilitator is not needed, so athletes can stretch on their own. This technique entails grasping one end of the rope/strap with both hands and attaching the other end to the appropriate area of the body (foot, ankle, elbow, etc.). From there, the athlete will pull on the rope/strap with the appropriate force to stretch the muscle.

Although a stretching rope/strap is relatively simple to use, a learning curve does exist. Therefore, softball players should seek out an experienced practitioner to help them master correct form before incorporating this equipment into their flexibility routine. If a rope or strap is not available, a rolled up towel can be used as a replacement.

Flexibility Program

The following *flexibility program* details a stretching regime that is appropriate for softball players. The entire routine can be accomplished in 10 to 15 minutes. It should be performed on a year-round basis, even during planned training breaks. As athletes progress and become more flexible, they should feel free to add and subtract stretches as they see fit.

1. *Knees to Chest*

- Lie flat on your back with your legs extended.

- Grasp your upper shins just below your kneecaps and pull your knees to your chest. Hold for 30 seconds.

- Alternate by pulling one leg at a time while keeping the other leg extended on the floor. Hold for 30 seconds.

- Perform two sets—one set with both legs and one set each with alternating legs.

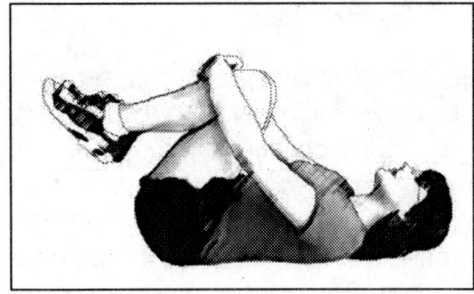 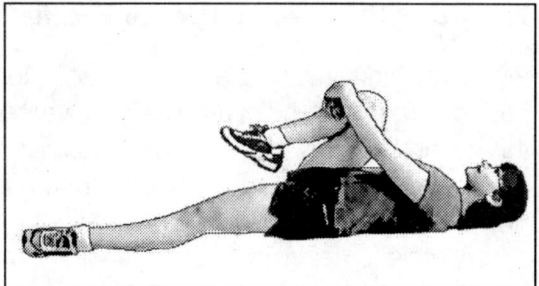

2. *Back Arch*

- Lie flat on your back with your legs extended.
- Flex your knees, sliding your feet toward your buttocks, and lift your pelvis off the floor, while arching your back.
- Perform one set. Hold in an arched position for 45 to 60 seconds.

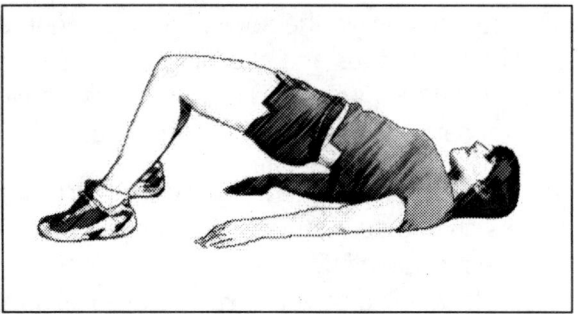

3. *Hip Flexor Stretch*

- Lie flat on your back with your knees flexed and your hands clasped behind your neck.
- Slowly lower both knees simultaneously to the floor, keeping your head, shoulders, and elbows flat on the floor. Hold at the bottom for 20 seconds.
- Perform two sets for each side.

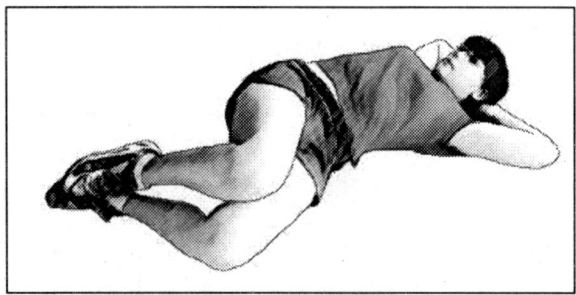

4. *Lying Hamstring Stretch*

- Lie flat on your back with your legs flexed and your heels close to the buttocks.
- Extend one leg upward and grasp underneath it. Then slowly pull it toward you while keeping the other leg as straight as possible. Hold for 30 seconds.
- Perform two sets with each leg.

5. *Reverse Plough*

- Lie facedown on the floor with your body extended.
- Place your palms on the floor between your chest and your hips.
- Press down evenly, and raise your head and trunk straight upward. Hold for 30 seconds.
- Perform two sets.

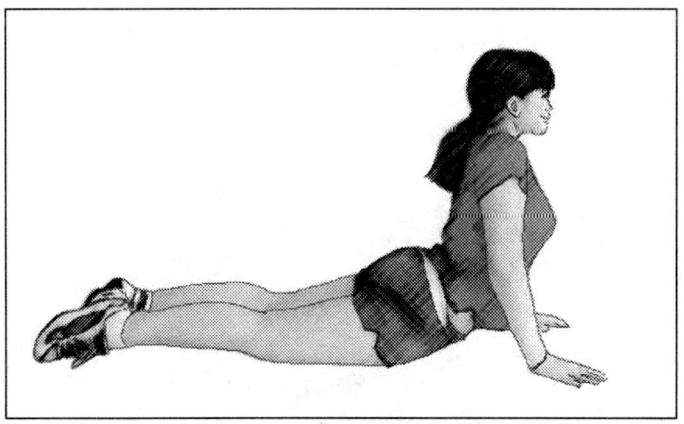

6. *Plough to Hamstring Stretch*

- Lie flat on your back with your arms on your hips.

- Raise both slightly bent legs up over your head and slowly lower your feet to the floor.

- After holding the stretch for 30 seconds, return under control to the seated position with your legs extended in front of you.

- Keeping both legs straight, bend forward at the waist and lower your trunk to your thighs, while simultaneously reaching your hands to your toes. Hold for 30 seconds.

- Perform two sets.

7. *Back/Quadriceps Stretch*

- Lie facedown on the floor with your body extended.

- Reach back and grab both ankles.

- Pull your ankles toward your upper back while at the same time lifting your chest off the floor.

- Perform one set. Hold for 45 seconds.

8. *Standing Groin Stretch*

- Stand with your legs spread approximately twice as wide as your shoulders.
- Bend straight down and attempt to touch your hands to the floor. Hold for 30 seconds.
- Perform two sets.

9. *Standing Quadriceps Stretch*

- Stand upright, bracing yourself with one hand against a wall for balance.
- Reach down and grasp one foot (right hand/right foot; left hand/left foot).
- Pull your heel to your buttocks and hold for 20 seconds.
- Perform two sets with each leg.

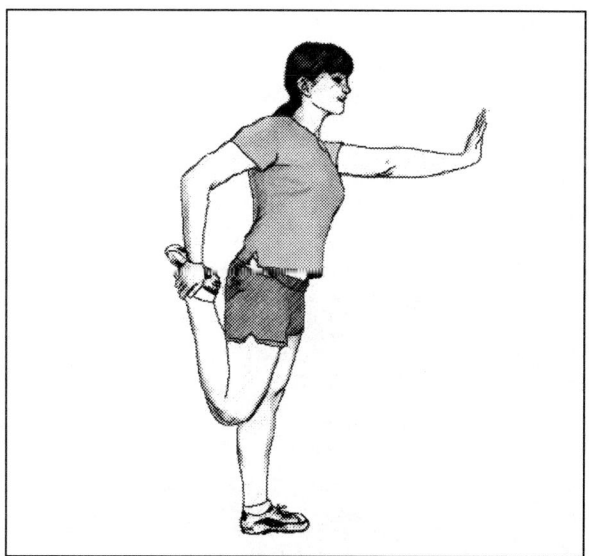

10. *Calf Stretch*

- Stand upright with both hands against a wall and your arms fully extended.
- Lean forward with your feet remaining flat on the floor, bending your arms and stretching your calves. Hold for 30 seconds.
- Perform two sets.

11. *Shoulder Stretch*

- Stand upright and cross one wrist over the other and interlock your hands.
- With your arms extended behind your head, shrug your shoulders upwards and reach toward the ceiling. Hold for 30 seconds.
- Perform two sets with hands clasped each way.

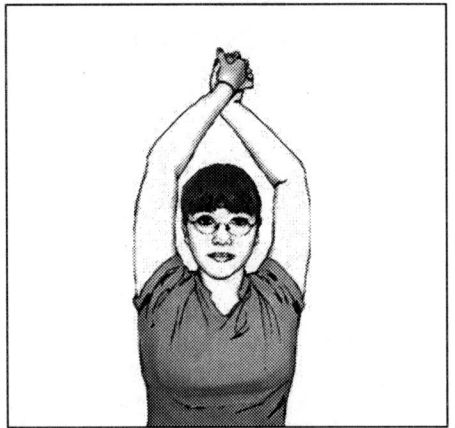

12. *Triceps Stretch*

- Sit or stand with one arm flexed and raised overhead next to your ear; rest your hand on your shoulder blade.

- Grasp your elbow with the opposite hand and pull it behind your head. Hold for 20 seconds.

- Perform two sets with each arm.

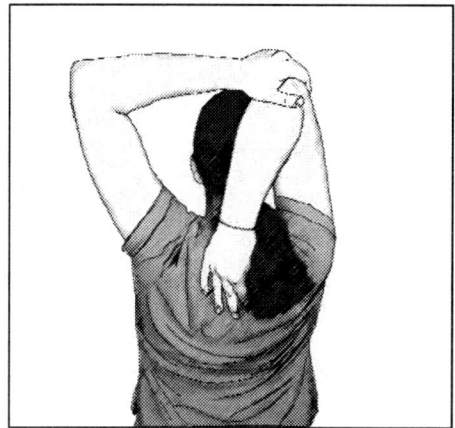

Pre-Movement Training Exercises

Prior to all movement-training workouts (plyometric, quickness/agility, speed, etc.), it is imperative that, along with the conventional warm-up and stretching activities, you perform the following series of pre-movement training exercises. These medium-intensity movements will set the stage for high-intensity training.

Exercise: Leg Swings

Execution: Stand sideways to a wall or bar and brace yourself against it with your inside hand. With your outside hand relaxed at your side and your outside leg planted firmly on the ground, swing your inside leg straight in front of your body and then back behind your body.

Sets and Repetitions: Two sets of 20 repetitions with each leg.

Exercise: Side Kicks

Execution: Stand facing a wall or bar and brace both of your slightly bent arms against it. You will be two to three feet away from the wall/bar depending on your height and the length of your arms. With your knee flexed slightly, proceed to swing your leg from side to side, while keeping your other leg planted firmly on the floor.

Sets and Repetitions: Two sets of 15 repetitions with each leg.

Exercise: Butt Kicks

Execution: Run straight ahead at an easy pace, attempting to kick your heels toward your buttocks.

Sets and Repetitions: Two sets of 20 to 30 yards.

Exercise: Body-Weight Side Lunge

Execution: Standing straight with your hands relaxed at your sides, step to the side, bend at the knees, and bring your back knee close to the floor. Proceed to drive yourself under control back to the standing position.

Sets and Repetitions: Two sets of 20 repetitions for each leg.

Exercise: Backpedals

Execution: With a slight forward lean and back straight, backpedal on the balls of your feet using short, quick strides. Your head should be up and your eyes fixed straight ahead.

Sets and Repetitions: Four sets of 12 to 15 yards.

Exercise: Carioca

Execution: Begin in an athletic stance—head up, back straight, legs spread slightly wider than shoulder width, and knees flexed. Proceed to step to the side with your left foot, followed by stepping behind your left foot with your right foot, simultaneously turning your hips in the direction you want to go. Then push your right leg powerfully in front of your left leg and continue in that pattern for the required distance. Change direction and repeat.

Sets and Repetitions: Four sets of 20 yards in each direction.

2

Recuperation, Overtraining, Attitude, and Injuries

If softball players hope to perform at peak levels on a year-round basis, they must take adequate time to recover between exercises, workouts, and training cycles; get sufficient amounts of sound sleep; avoid overtraining; maintain a positive attitude; and deal conscientiously with injuries. The following are a few ways to achieve these objectives.

Recuperation

Giving your body the opportunity to adequately recover from the rigors of training is a prerequisite for success on the softball field. Unfortunately, recuperation is a very tricky subject, since no two athletes have exactly the same recovery needs. Some are able to bounce back very quickly from even the most strenuous workouts, while others get the most out of their conditioning programs by employing maximum rest intervals between exercise bouts. Still others, the majority, fall somewhere in-between. Needless to say, proper recuperation necessitates a very individual and delicate balance.

Now that you know how diverse recovery requirements among athletes can be, how do you go about finding what yours are? The first and most important step is to take personal responsibility. Although coaches, trainers, well-meaning parents, and more experienced teammates can steer you in the right direction, you ultimately should develop an intuitive feel for when to push ahead with hard training and when to prudently scale back your workouts. Fortunately, this instinctive feel comes with experience, and as you progress as an athlete, your recovery needs will become second nature. Most elite athletes who've been training for many years can tell day to day whether their bodies are best served by more or less work. Down the road, you will be able to do the same.

Sleep

The founder of a popular sports camp once said, "If you want to soar with the eagles in the daytime, you can't hoot with the owls at night." As a hard-training softball player, you must get adequate sleep and rest if you hope to perform at your best. Sleep requirements vary from person to person. Some individuals are able to get by on only five or six hours per night with no ill effects, while others need up to 10 hours every night to feel fully rested. Most active softball players will require seven-and-a-half to eight hours of sound sleep per night. Younger athletes (under 18 years of age) will usually need more sleep than their older counterparts. Short naps (20 to 30 minutes) in the middle of the day can help to rejuvenate you and are suggested if you have the time and inclination. Longer naps (two to three hours) tend to cause grogginess and should be avoided, especially on the day of a game.

Sleep researchers suggest waking up at the same time every day regardless of when you turned in is helpful in developing a regular sleep pattern. This practice may be difficult at times, especially after a late night game or when traveling, but this strategy is proven for enhancing the quality of sleep and should be adhered to whenever possible. Coffee and other highly caffeinated drinks, such as colas and teas, should be kept to a minimum, especially late in the day, as these products can cause insomnia. Warm milk and soft cheeses consumed close to bedtime can sometimes improve the quality of your sleep, as can taking a warm bath or whirlpool two to three hours prior to retiring.

Two notoriously difficult times for athletes to garner a good night's sleep are the night before an important game and the night after participating in a late day or night game. The key to sleeping well the night before an important event, say a softball playoff game, is more mental than physical. This mental aspect does not mean you shouldn't follow the previous suggestions, such as taking a warm bath, drinking some warm milk, and avoiding caffeinated beverages close to bedtime. But, getting your mind off tomorrow's responsibilities is the real secret to entering pre-game night dreamland.

After practice is concluded and the final preparations have been discussed, you should stop thinking about the following day's game. Go to a movie, read a non-softball related book, watch some mindless television, or do anything else so you don't focus on the upcoming game. Remember, thinking incessantly about what you're going to do on the field the next day will do absolutely nothing to improve your performance. In fact, the sleep you sacrifice by obsessing about your duties will actually hinder your ability to execute.

The proposition of sleeping after a late day or night competition is even more challenging. After a late game, you will not only encounter the psychological aspect of dwelling on your performance, which many athletes describe as a movie that continues repeating itself frame-by-frame, over-and-over, and then over again, but the physical ramifications will manifest as well.

Coping with the mental side of sleeping after games basically mirrors that of pregame nights. But, instead of endeavoring to keep your mind off what you're going to do on the field, you'll be trying to block out repetitively re-living what you've just accomplished in-between the lines. Use the same methods described previously, or any others you might think of, to refrain from dwelling on your game performance, whether your performance was good, bad, or mediocre. Easier said than done, of course, but necessary if you hope to attain that elusive postgame shut eye.

The physiological aspect of sleeping after late day or night games also requires attention. Your body will be in overdrive after an intense competition. Game play elicits a high level of adrenaline flow, which unfortunately doesn't leave your body when the final out is made. For your system to get back to its normal state can literally take hours. However, implementing some proven strategies will contribute to cycling your body down after a hard fought competition. Three of the most helpful strategies are detailed in the following section.

Engage in a Comprehensive Postgame Cool-Down

As discussed in Chapter 1, cooling down efficiently after intense physical activity is extremely important. Subsequent to a late day or night game, cooling down is absolutely critical, especially when it comes to getting a good night's rest. Following the cool-down protocol discussed in Chapter 1 should help you considerably in your quest for sound postgame slumber.

Hit the Weight Room after Competition

Heading to the weight room immediately following a game is not only a great way to stay current with your in-season strength program, but it will contribute to pumping some of that nervous energy and adrenaline out of your system. Postgame strength workouts are discussed in detail in Chapter 10.

Eat a Healthy, Filling Postgame Meal

After a game, a number of hours will have passed since you've last eaten. (Most pregame meals take place three to four hours before competition.) Going to bed on an empty stomach after competition is a sure ticket to disrupted sleep—not to mention leaving your energy depleted for the following day's activities.

Overtraining

Being in an overtrained state is the *enemy* of any athlete. It hinders progress, inhibits performance, and can lead to injury. As a softball player engaging in a full slate of conditioning disciplines, you must remain acutely aware of how your body is responding to the stresses of intense physical activity. Not doing so will greatly increase your chances of becoming overtrained.

You'll find both good news and bad news on the overtraining front. First, the bad news: no one, regardless of how experienced they are with their training, has ever achieved the absolute perfect balance between training and rest. To some extent, despite the advances in training technology, learning individual exercise tolerance is still as much an art as a science. The good news, however, is that by following the principles detailed in *Peak Conditioning Training for Softball*, your chances of becoming overtrained are slim. The following points provide a list of common symptoms of overtraining, as well as some proven remedies if your body does become overtrained.

Symptoms

- Increased muscle, joint, and tendon soreness
- Noticeable loss of strength, power, and conditioning
- A preponderance of minor injuries
- Lack of enthusiasm for workouts
- Irritability
- Insomnia

Remedies

- Take a training break (one to two weeks).
- Decrease workout intensity.
- Change up your workout routine.
- Include some extra stretching and warm-up/cool-down activities in your workouts.
- Learn from past mistakes.

Off-Season Overtraining—More Prevalent Than You Think

When most athletes think of overtraining, they think in-season, right? After all, during the season is when you are competing in games, engaging in intense team practices, adhering to rigorous school schedules, and dealing with the relentless pressure of winning and losing.

While overtraining certainly does occur during the competitive season, believe it or not, overtraining is actually more prevalent in the off-season. Why? Following are a few of the reasons.

Lack of day-to-day supervision: Think about it. During the regular campaign, you are monitored by coaches, trainers, and conditioning specialists for signs of physical breakdown. Practice time and intensity, travel, strength/conditioning workouts, and rest intervals are all carefully planned so you don't over do it.

On the other hand, in the off-season, unless you employ a full-time personal trainer (which is financially out of the question for most), you are basically left to your own devices when it comes to softball and training related activities. Some coaches may provide you with a written off-season workout plan, but rarely will they be physically present to supervise your workouts. This lack of guidance is the major cause for off-season overtraining by softball players and other athletes.

Numerous training modalities: A dizzying array of training options are available to today's athletes. Plyometrics (an advanced form of explosiveness training), high intensity weightlifting, and imaginative speed training are just a few of the more challenging. Many dedicated athletes are tempted to put full effort and time into all aspects of their training. This practice, while commendable, is a recipe for overtraining.

In order to reach your full potential on the softball field and avoid off-season overtraining, you must deal efficiently with the wide variety of workout choices at your disposal. One way to do this is to combine training modalities. For example, plyometric and agility workouts can be combined, as can speed training and certain cross training options such as jumping rope or stadium step running. This approach will ensure adequate rest and recuperation between high intensity training sessions.

Pressure to be in top shape year round: One of the few negatives to the sports fitness boom is the pressure it puts on young athletes to maintain top physical conditioning on a year-round basis. Off-season leagues and camps, non-sanctioned workouts for coaches and scouts, and the striving to be in top condition for the commencement of team practice contribute to athletes becoming overtrained in the off-season. Keeping your off-season workouts and responsibilities to reasonable levels is important. This practice will allow you to improve optimally and, most importantly, be ready when it counts in the regular season.

Maintain a Positive Attitude

Softball is a game of ups and downs. Base hits and diving catches are interspersed with strikeouts and errors. No matter how talented you are or how hard you work at the game, success and failure will follow you on to the softball field.

The same holds true in your softball strength and conditioning program. Not all workouts are created equal. Some will be satisfying and progressive. Others will be below par and disappointing. Sticking points in your training, minor injuries, and unexpected changes in schedule are frustrating realities for all athletes.

Your ability to bounce back from bad games and workouts is a key factor to your ultimate success on the softball field. Learning how to transcend your circumstances and maintain a positive, improvement-conscious attitude is of paramount importance for all players. Presented next are some tips for keeping your attitude positive when things aren't going your way.

Be Aware: Being mindful of your disappointments and frustrations is essential. You may have left the tying run on base, lost a close pitching decision, or skipped a conditioning workout, but the specific transgression does not matter. Being aware will help you to deal with adversity immediately and to move forward quickly.

Analyze Briefly: *Briefly* analyze and learn what you can from your failure and move on. Dwelling on your mistakes is a waste of time and energy. Approaching your ups and downs on the field in this manner will contribute to making you a clear-minded, and ultimately better, softball player.

Focus on the Next Thing: Focusing intently on your next task after experiencing a disappointment, whether it be your subsequent at bat, workout, or practice, is crucial to maintaining a positive attitude. Many top athletes from a variety of sports find that setting their minds "forward" is the best way to move past a failure and proceed to performing at their best.

Remember, Nobody's Perfect: Most dedicated athletes demand a lot of themselves. They work hard and strive for perfection. However, striving for perfection is one thing; expecting perfection is quite another. Perfection is not a human trait. Even the most exemplary athletes experience failure and make mistakes, usually quite often. So, by all means, strive to be the best you can be, but always remember that nobody's perfect on the softball field—or anywhere else for that matter.

Injury Prevention

Injury prevention is a key to a long and successful athletic career. Softball players, as is the case with all serious athletes, are prone to numerous competition and workout related injuries. Sprained ankles, twisted knees, pulled hamstrings, strained shoulders, and hyperextended elbows, you name the ailment, and at one time or another most competitive softball players have experienced them. Fortunately, the incidence of these injuries and others like them can be curtailed. The secret is to condition your body to its fullest potential.

By following the suggestions and training programs in *Peak Conditioning Training for Softball*, you can greatly reduce your risk of injury. Warming up and cooling down properly, improving and maintaining flexibility, and adhering to a balanced nutritional plan all contribute substantially to preventing injury, as does executing proper running form, mastering correct footwork, and balancing your training with a variety of exercise choices.

Of all aspects of physical conditioning, strength training is perhaps the most integral component to prevent injury. The additional strength and muscle tissue you build around your joints act as shock absorbers during high-impact activities (such as sliding into second base, landing during plyometric drills, or running full-speed into an outfield fence) and as a stress reducer during repetitive actions (i.e., pitching, swinging, jogging, etc.). A strong lower back and mid-section stave off a variety of lower back ailments, including a frustrating condition called sciatica, which gives rise to pain extending from the lower back to the lower leg and foot. Anyone who has experienced this injury knows how important prevention is, because once sciatica occurs this condition can become chronic and long lasting, not to mention extremely painful.

Finally, always aspire to maintain an awareness of how your body feels from day to day, especially during the long, grueling softball season. Minor aches and pains, while inevitable, can often be precursors to full-blown injuries. Recognizing these kinks and acting immediately and appropriately (extra rest, special treatment in the training room, additional warm-up/cool-down, etc.) can help you avoid many injuries before they manifest.

In the competitive world of softball, remaining healthy and at full strength for extended periods of time can mean the difference between success and failure for both players and teams. Those athletes who condition themselves optimally have the best chance of playing peak performance softball week after week, month after month, and year after year without injury getting in the way.

Special Note for All Female Athletes

The subject of female athletes and knee injuries deserves much attention and emphasis, since *Peak Conditioning Training for Softball* is devoted to the improvement of female athletes.

The preponderance of serious knee injuries, especially the dreaded anterior cruciate ligament (ACL) tear, among female athletes is alarming. One recent study showed that female college basketball players are as much as seven times more likely to tear their ACLs during competition as their male counterparts. This large discrepancy has yielded numerous theories as to why this occurs. Many in the medical community believe that because of their wider hip structure; looser, weaker, and smaller ligaments; and generally weaker hamstring muscles; females are more susceptible to knee injuries.

Regardless of the reasons, the fact that ACL tears are extremely painful and debilitating is beyond debate. ACL tears can keep you out of action for extended periods of time, sometimes up to a year, and, in many instances, will contribute to future deterioration of the knee joint. In addition, once you sustain a serious knee injury, the chances of re-injury to the area increases many-fold.

The best defense against these incapacitating injuries is, as they say, a good offense. A good offense in this case refers to proper and aggressive training. Knee injury prevention programs should include a combination of balance exercises performed mostly unilaterally (on one leg) and a variety of lower body strengthening movements that focus on the core muscles of the hips and upper legs, with an emphasis on the hamstrings. Learning and adhering to proper running and landing techniques, maintaining an ideal body weight relative to your frame, improving flexibility, and achieving optimal levels of physical conditioning will also help curtail the incidence of knee injuries.

ACL tears and other dynamic knee injuries occur more frequently in sports such as soccer and field hockey where repetitive, explosive changes of direction are prevalent. Nevertheless, all female athletes, including each and every softball player, should engage in some form of knee injury prevention program. Following the balance and lower body strength training protocols in *Peak Conditioning Training for Softball* will substantially lower your chances of experiencing a serious knee injury such as an ACL tear.

Injury Rehabilitation

Despite the high level of conditioning most softball players attain today, injuries are still an inevitable part of the game. The repetitive actions of throwing, swinging, and running, combined with the impact absorbed from diving for balls on hard infields, getting hit by a pitches, along with other various and sundry collisions with teammates and opponents, make it virtually impossible for even the most highly conditioned athletes to escape injury forever. Because of this reality, the remainder of this chapter includes injury rehabilitation tips that should make your journey from injury back to the field a little easier. Keep in mind, however, that the following information is not meant in any way to take the place of consulting and working closely with experienced medical and rehabilitation personnel.

• *Let them know*: When you sustain an injury of any kind, the first step is to immediately communicate with the appropriate personnel (trainers, coaches, doctors, etc.). A clear and succinct explanation of your injury is crucial for proper diagnosis and a key to a quick recovery. Doctors and trainers, while experienced in dealing with injured athletes, are not mind readers. Being as precise as possible when describing your injury will go a long way toward ensuring that the suitable treatment/rehabilitation protocol will be prescribed.

• *Choose the right physical therapist*: Once a doctor has examined you, it is time to go about the process of choosing a physical therapist to help you rehabilitate. While most college programs have trained rehabilitation personnel on staff, the large majority of high schools and junior high schools do not. Therefore, it may very well be up to you.

The first step in choosing a physical therapist involves seeking recommendations, particularly from those individuals who've experienced a similar injury to yours and followed it up with a successful rehabilitation. Your coaches and athletic trainers may also be able to suggest respected physical therapists in your area.

Next, after you've narrowed down the therapist candidates to two or three, set up a visit with each one. This will allow you to not only get a feel for the therapist's style, but assess the facilities as well. When evaluating the facilities, pay particular attention to the atmosphere, since rehabilitation workouts will take all the enthusiasm you can muster.

Finally, once you've made the choice, stick with it. Switching physical therapists in midstream will cause a major disruption in your rehabilitation training. Unless the fit with the therapist is just untenable, stay the course and continue to work with your original choice.

- *Be consistent*: Consistency is an essential factor in any progressive strength and conditioning program. Injury rehabilitation is no different. Missing treatment and/or rehab sessions even periodically is not an option for the competitive softball player. If your goal after sustaining an injury is to get back on the field at full strength as soon as possible, adhering to a consistent rehabilitation schedule is a must. Remember, consistency plus hard work equals a successful rehabilitation.

- *Patience*: Your patience will be severely tested when coming back from an injury. During the rehabilitation process, patience is not only a virtue but an absolute necessity. Like it or not (and you probably won't), the body has its own timetable for recovery independent of your opinion about it. It only responds to the proper ratio of exercise, treatment, and rest spread over the appropriate period of time. Realizing this need for patience early on will save you much anguish and frustration.

- *Don't come back too soon*: Although you will surely be tempted (all dedicated athletes are), coming back to action before you're ready is a major mistake, one that will put you at risk of re-injury. The list of high-profile athletes who return too soon from injury only to re-injure themselves would fill this book many times over. Regardless of the outside pressures you may experience from coaches, teammates, and family members, make sure to keep your own counsel and take all the time you need for recovery and rehabilitation before jumping back into the competitive fray. In the long run, this approach will be best for both you and your team.

- *Injury rehabilitation never really ends*: Once you return to full strength after rehabilitating from an injury, the special attention given to the injured area is not over.

Continuing to monitor your former injury for signs off aggravation and pain is imperative. These sensations may be precursors to re-injury and should be dealt with immediately and appropriately (rest, treatment, extra flexibility work, etc.). You may also need to keep up with at least some extra strength training for the region. For example, if you're coming off a knee injury where substantial weakness and muscle atrophy occurred, engaging in a few extra sets of post rehab strength exercise each workout for the formally injured leg is in order.

3

Softball Nutrition

Nutrition has never been a simple subject. These days, however, it has become downright confusing. Foods that only a few short years ago were considered nutritious and healthy are now, according to some, to be avoided at all cost. Other foods, labeled the devils of the nutritional world for decades, currently stand as the darlings of the diet set.

What is an improvement conscious softball player to do in this contentious and ever-changing environment? The advice in this book is simple and can be summed up in two short words: *stay balanced*. A balanced diet, complete with ample complex carbohydrates, reasonable amounts of high-quality protein, adequate fat intake, and plenty of water, is still the ticket to high performance in-between the lines.

This chapter will take you through the mine field that has become sports nutrition. It begins with the components of balanced nutrition, including the controversial subjects of dietary supplements and so-called performance-enhancing drugs, continues with weight control strategies, and concludes with sample meal plans that softball players can incorporate on a year-round basis.

Components of Balanced Nutrition

Water

Approximately two-thirds of your body mass is composed of water. It is without question the most important ingredient in any athlete's diet. Water performs many functions in the body, including lubricating joints, modulating body temperature (a key factor during vigorous exercise), carrying nutrients to cells and waste products away from cells, and helping the digestion and absorption of food.

Drinking a minimum of eight 12-ounce glasses of water each day is imperative. On hot humid days, or when exorbitant amounts of energy are expended such as during two-a-day preseason workouts, up to 12 12-ounce glasses should be consumed. Other liquids such as lemonade, various fruit juices, and sports drinks like Gatorade basically have the same effect as water. (All are water based.) Vegetables and fresh fruits also contain substantial amounts of water. Pure water is still the simplest (and least expensive) way to stay hydrated, however. Alcoholic, caffeinated, and carbonated beverages should be avoided as much as possible, as they include ingredients that actually contribute to dehydration. Always make sure to keep your fluid intake high before, during, and after exercise sessions, as well as consistent throughout the day. To help accomplish this, it is suggested that you carry a filled water bottle with you from morning to night. Remaining optimally hydrated contributes to buoyant health and peak athletic performance. Make it part of your lifestyle.

Carbohydrates (% of total calories = 55% to 60%. Calories per gram = 4)

Carbohydrates are the easiest form of food for the body to turn into energy. They are, however, not all created equal. Complex carbohydrates, which include potatoes, rice, vegetables, beans, breads, and pastas, provide long-term energy and are easily digested. These foods contain necessary nutrients such as B vitamins and should be the mainstay of your softball nutritional plan. Complex carbohydrates will also always be the primary part of your pre-game or pre-workout meal. Simple carbohydrates, such as fruits and processed sugars, while easily digested, provide only short-term energy. With the exception of fresh fruit and some fruit juices, which provide excellent sources of important nutrients (minerals, fiber, vitamins) and do not rapidly lower blood sugar levels, simple carbohydrates should be eaten only in moderation.

How many grams of carbohydrates should be consumed per day is a function of your activity level and individual metabolism. As a rule of thumb, when engaging in heavy training multiply your body weight by five to derive the appropriate number of carbohydrate grams to be eaten each day. During light training intervals or over training breaks use three as the multiplier. As mentioned previously, these are just approximations and much will depend on the speed of your individual metabolism. It is best to get a feel through trial and error for how your body responds to different amounts of food and proceed to act (and eat) accordingly.

Proteins (% of total calories = 25% to 30%. Calories per gram = 4)

Protein is used by the body to build and repair muscle tissue. Obviously, hard-training softball players who are engaging in physically demanding activities such as weightlifting and speed training should include ample amounts of protein in their diets. The best sources of protein are eggs, fish, red meat, poultry (chicken, turkey, etc.), and diary products. These foods are referred to as complete proteins, since they contain all the amino acids necessary to build muscle. Incomplete proteins, such as most plant proteins, lack one or more of the essential amino acids and can only contribute to the muscle building process if consumed in the proper combinations. Food combining, such as eating beans together with rice, experienced a good deal of popularity some years back as a way to get adequate protein without the saturated fat present in animal proteins. However, this practice has fallen out of favor to some extent because the combining process is not easy to follow when you're not preparing your own food. Unless you are involved in a weight-gaining program (as explained later in the chapter), eating approximately .50 to .60 grams of protein daily per pound of body weight should be sufficient for a competitive softball player.

Fats (% of total calories = 15% to 20%. Calories per gram = 9)

Fats, similar to carbohydrates and proteins, are needed by the body. They supply a major source of energy, protect vital organs, and help to prevent starvation during times of insufficient food intake. The problem is that the average American, including many competitive athletes, derives up to 50% percent of her calories from fat. While the once popular extremely low-fat diet is not suggested here, neither is the 50-percent fat diet. This amount of fat consumption can add unwanted weight to the physique and raise cholesterol levels, which increases the risk of heart disease. To keep your fat intake low, make a conscious effort to stay away from fried foods, fatty meats, and high-fat dairy food (ice cream, whole milk, etc.). The best low-fat sources of protein include fresh fish, egg whites, skim or 1% milk, lean read meats, and poultry.

Vitamins

Vitamins perform a variety of important functions. For example, vitamin D assists in the absorption of calcium and vitamin C enhances resistance to infection. While vitamins are not a source of energy, they do release energy from the food you eat. Vitamins are only needed by the body in small amounts and can, for the most part, be obtained from eating a balanced, nutritionally sound diet with limited supplementation.

Two types of vitamin classifications exist: water-soluble (B and C) and fat-soluble (A, D, E, and K). Water-soluble vitamins are not stored in the body. Therefore, extra amounts are flushed from the system easily. On the other hand, fat-soluble vitamins are stored in the body's fat and can be toxic if excessive amounts are ingested.

Minerals

More than 20 mineral elements are found in the body, 17 of which are necessary in your diet. Some of the most important minerals include calcium, iron, copper, iodine, magnesium, manganese, phosphorus, potassium, and zinc. Minerals help to build strong bones, maintain bodily tissues, and help muscles work efficiently. Most minerals that your body requires can be obtained by eating a balanced diet.

However, women may want to consider supplementing their diets with extra calcium and iron. Calcium in the diet helps to prevent osteoporosis, which is much more common in women than in men. Ingesting adequate calcium is especially important during the years of 12 to 16 when the bone structure is developing. Active women of menstrual age need to keep their iron intake reasonably high (about 18 milligrams per day) or risk developing iron deficiency anemia, which has been known to cause performance deficits in athletes.

Nutritional Supplements

The vast array of nutritional supplements available today is mind-boggling. Some promise to build massive amounts of strength and muscle. Others claim to burn fat, making bodies lean and muscularly defined. Still others, like the popular supplement creatine, are said to improve sports and workout performance.

Regardless of whether you personally believe the previous claims or not, one thing is beyond debate: nutritional supplements are big business. Sales are estimated at 50 million annually and growing rapidly. Many of the dollars are spent by young athletes looking for that elusive competitive edge. The major reason for the popularity of nutritional supplements among youngsters, other than the aggressive marketing efforts by the supplement manufactures, is their well documented use by superstar athletes, such as Barry Bonds, debatably major league baseball's all-time greatest player. Bonds credits some of his late career success on the field and in the weight room to the use of nutritional supplements.

Despite their widespread use and popularity, the jury is still out as to how much benefit dietary supplements actually provide. Many experts in the nutritional field believe that if you're eating a well-balanced, nutritionally sound diet, your need for supplementation is minimal. Taking a multi-vitamin is fine, as is snacking on an energy bar prior to a workout or competition, but the other things, such as protein powders, so-called mega-mass tablets, and fat-burning pills and drinks, are mostly a waste of money and are more likely to produce stomach cramps and insomnia than they are to improve softball performance. In fact, an extra helping of egg whites and a little less late night pizza will help build muscle and reduce fat more effectively than the majority of these expensive, well-promoted products.

Before concluding this section, you should be aware of two popular dietary supplements that you may want to consider incorporating into your diet. The first, glucosamine chondroitin, has shown to substantially lesson joint soreness, particularly in the knee and shoulder regions, two extremely important areas of the body for softball players. This product is highly touted throughout Europe and has begun to draw a large following in the United States in recent years as well. The best news of all concerning glucosamine chondroitin is that no harmful side affects are apparent.

Consuming glucosamine chondroitin regularly, especially for those athletes recovering from any type of joint injury/surgery, is strongly suggested. The dosage recommendations vary somewhat, but two to three pills per day containing a combination of 1500 mg. of glucosamine and 1200 mg. of chondroitin should be about right for hard training softball players. This product is widely available at drug stores and nutritional product stores.

The second popular supplement worth special mention, creatine, seems to have performance-enhancing merit. Creatine is a natural substance manufactured in the body and serves as a small energy source, assisting in the execution of explosive, short-duration activities such as swinging a bat and dynamic weightlifting. According to proponents, adding or loading creatine into the system will enhance an athlete's ability to perform explosive actions. Be aware that creatine supplementation does not actually build muscle; it allows you to work out harder, with the byproduct being more strength and muscular development.

The rate at which creatine is generated in the body is approximately two grams per day. Recommended supplementation guidelines call for four to six grams daily for five days (loading phase), followed by two grams per day thereafter (maintenance phase). Creatine usually comes in powered form and should be mixed with water or fruit juice (grape juice is most popular) for ingestion.

If you do decide to supplement your diet with creatine, consuming extra water is imperative. This practice may help limit cramping, which is a common complaint among regular creatine users. Keep in mind that while the correct way to use creatine was previously discussed, it is not meant to be construed as a full endorsement of the product. Creatine has been researched and studied more than most nutritional supplements; however, many professionals in the medical community still feel that more needs to be learned about its long-term effects. Before engaging in a creatine supplementation program, you should consult your physician.

Steroids and Other Performance-Enhancing Drugs

When most people think of steroids or performance-enhancing drug use, muscular male athletes usually come to mind. However, over the years numerous female athletes, mostly track and field competitors and swimmers, have also been linked to steroids and similar drugs.

Regardless of gender, experimenting even casually with these substances is a recipe for disaster and is strongly discouraged. While some short-term benefits may occur, such as increased muscle size and strength, the risks greatly outweigh the rewards. The list of harmful side effects is lengthy and frightening. Some of the most serious are as follows:

- Liver cancer
- Muscle pulls and tears
- High blood pressure
- Joint problems
- Increased risk of heart disease
- Irritability
- Impaired immune system
- Excessive aggressiveness

    Other less dangerous side effects of special concern to women include a deepening of the voice, acne on the shoulders and back, and a distinct change in facial features. And if all the side effects is not enough to discourage you from dabbling with these dangerous drugs, be aware that steroids and their brethren are illegal, and possessing them, in even small amounts, could land you in some serious legal jeopardy. Obviously, softball and performance-enhancing drugs don't mix. Case closed.

Weight Control

Softball players have a variety of reasons for wanting to gain or lose weight. Some may need to increase their physical strength in order to hit for more power, thus requiring some additional muscular body weight. Others desire to lose weight in order to increase their speed, quickness, and endurance. In either case, athletes should take care to work within their genetic make-up and body type (i.e., ectomorph: slim build; mesomorph: muscular build; endomorph: heavy/large build; etc.) and aspire to maintain a reasonably low level of body fat, which will be somewhere between 12 to 18 percent for active female athletes.

Weight Gain

In order to gain weight in a safe and efficient manner, you should focus on two major factors. First, you must take in more calories than you expend—not always that easy for a hard-training softball player. Second, you should engage in a year-round strength training program that focuses on building maximum muscle mass. This approach will ensure that the weight you gain comes in the form of lean muscle tissue and not unwanted fat.

    Always keep in mind that being in the weight-gaining mode doesn't necessarily mean you have clearance to eat anything and everything in your path. Your fat consumption should still remain moderate, and overstuffing yourself with starchy carbohydrates is strongly discouraged. Adding large amounts of body fat will inhibit performance, appearance, and health. On the other hand, small amounts of extra protein should be added to your diet during a weight gain cycle. As was discussed previously in this chapter, proteins are the building blocks of muscle, and you must consume enough protein if you hope to gain lean body weight. However, limits exist. The body can only metabolize 30 to 35 grams of protein (approximately one-and-a-half cans of tuna) at any given time. The best way to maximize protein into your diet is to incorporate five to six reasonably small meals spread three-to-four hours apart over the course of a day.

Weight Loss

For softball players who wish to lose weight, the first point to be aware of is that the scale should never be the ultimate judge. This may be difficult for today's young women who were brought up to respect the scale. As mentioned previously, every individual has a unique build, and playing weight is not nearly as important as body composition (relative amounts of muscle, bone, and fat in the body). Overweight athletes should always make losing fat and gaining lean muscle tissue their number one priority. Since muscle weighs more than fat, what you actually weigh is far less important than how it is distributed throughout the body. The majority of top-level athletes, including most world-class softball players, would be considered overweight by American medical body weight charts. These charts and standards mean nothing to competitive athletes and should be ignored.

Numerous strategies can be implemented to lower your body composition. Some of the most time-tested are as follows:

- Eat five to six smaller meals per day as opposed to the traditional three larger ones.

- Avoid eating heavy late at night before retiring. This means (unfortunately) no midnight snacks or late night pizza binges.

- Eat high-fiber, reasonably low fat meals regularly.

- Starchy carbohydrates such as potatoes, pastas, and white breads should be moderated. Remember, however, that hard-training softball players need energy to perform and workout, so it is recommended not to reduce starchy carbohydrates drastically.

- Get the majority of your protein from low-fat sources such as fish, lean meats, poultry, and egg whites.

- Avoid fried foods.

- Drink ample amounts of water throughout the day to flush your system.

- In addition to keeping your food intake moderate, engage in some form of aerobic exercise on a regular basis.

- Stay current with your strength program. Building lean muscle tissue will help your body burn fat more efficiently.

- Stay clear of fad diets and diet pills. These never work in the long run and can cause health problems.
- Lose fat/weight gradually.

Many Female Athletes Don't Eat Enough

Before ending this section on weight loss, it is important that a reoccurring problem in the women's sports world is discussed. Among many competitive female athletes, recent studies have shown that energy intake appeared to be lower than energy expenditure: a sure sign that not enough calories are being consumed. Even more alarming was the fact that a large percentage of female team sport athletes were found to be trying to lose weight unnecessarily during their seasons. Dieting during the competitive season is highly discouraged unless a serious weight problem exists, one that compromises your health or severely inhibits your on-field performance. In fact, most softball players should attempt to stabilize their in-season weight so as not to lose strength and power. (Most high-level athletes, regardless of the sport, tend to lose weight during their competitive campaigns.)

Sample Meal Plans

Pre-Game Meal

Years ago a pre-game meal for softball players may have consisted of a 12-ounce well-done steak, a baked potato piled high with butter and sour cream, and, if you were lucky, a small serving of some type of vegetable. Eating a high-protein, high-fat pre-game meal was the tradition. What the sports nutrition community has learned (thankfully) over the years is that fatty foods take a substantial amount of energy to digest, thus causing energy depletion in the body, cramping, and general discomfort. Not exactly what softball players are looking for prior to a game.

A pre-game meal for softball players should include ample portions of complex carbohydrates, very little protein and fat, and large amounts of hydrating liquids. As mentioned earlier in this chapter, complex carbohydrates such as pasta and rice are easily digested and, when broken down, produce glucose, which supplies the body's energy needs. Before intense physical exertion, such as a softball game or conditioning workout, having large amounts of energy at your disposal is obviously crucial. Pre-game meals should be planned three-and-a-half hours or so before competition.

Tables 3-1 through 3-5 detail sample meal plans for softball players. Keep in mind that the following meal suggestions described are meant to be a basic guide only. What diet plan you ultimately use will depend on numerous factors, including food tastes, individual metabolism, activity level, and health variables.

- Three-quarter cup of oatmeal with sliced half banana and three ounces of 1% milk
- Four medium-sized whole wheat pancakes with maple syrup
- 12-ounce glass of orange juice
- 12-ounce glass of water

Table 3-1. Sample pre-game meal (afternoon game)

- Large bowl of whole wheat pasta (approximately five ounces) with marinara sauce
- Large mixed salad with low-fat dressing
- Half a banana with peanut butter
- 12-ounce glass of Gatorade
- 12-ounce glass of water

Table 3-2. Sample pre-game meal (night game)

Breakfast:	Three-egg (two yolks) western omelet
	Two slices of dry whole wheat or whole grain bread
	One-half cup bowl of oatmeal with raisins and three ounces of 2% milk
	12-ounce glass of grapefruit juice
	12-ounce glass of water
Lunch:	Large turkey sandwich on rye bread with lettuce, tomato and mustard
	Medium-sized bowl of vegetable soup
	Two 12-ounce glasses of water
Mid-Afternoon Snack:	Five whole wheat crackers spread with peanut butter
	12-ounce glass of apple juice
Dinner:	Large piece of grilled fish (salmon, tuna, halibut, or swordfish)
	Baked potato with low-fat sour cream
	Medium mixed salad with Italian dressing
	Small slice of pound cake
	Two 12-ounce glasses of water

Table 3-3. Sample daily meal plan for softball players

Breakfast:	Two poached eggs on one large slice of whole wheat or whole grain bread
	Medium-sized bowl of cold cereal (Cheerios, Total, or Special K) with 1% milk
	12-ounce glass of grape juice
	12-ounce glass of water
Lunch:	Large chef salad with Italian dressing
	Medium-sized whole wheat roll (dry)
	Two 12-ounce glasses of water
Dinner:	12-ounce cut of lean beef
	Small servings of broccoli and cauliflower
	3-ounce bowl of whole wheat pasta with olive oil dressing
	Two 12-ounce glasses of water
P.M. Snack:	One slice of pound cake with strawberries
	12-ounce glass of 2% milk

Table 3-4. Sample daily meal plan for softball players

Breakfast:	Four scrambled eggs (two yolks) with two slices of pumpernickel toast
	One-half cup of oatmeal with two tablespoons of wheat germ
	12-ounce glass of orange juice
	12-ounce glass of water
Lunch:	Two medium-sized chicken breasts
	One-cup serving of brown rice
	Medium serving of grilled vegetables
	Two 12-ounce glasses of water
Mid-Afternoon Snack:	Medium serving of mixed nuts with dried fruit
	12-ounce glass of water
Dinner:	6-ounce bowl of whole wheat pasta with shrimp topped with marinara sauce
	Medium-sized mixed salad topped with hard cheese slices and Italian dressing
	Small container of low-fat yogurt
	Two 12-ounce glasses of water

Table 3-5. Sample daily meal plan for softball players

PART II
SOFTBALL CONDITIONING

4

Softball Conditioning Basics

This chapter will cover all aspects of softball conditioning. But before moving on to the specifics, it is important that you have at least a fundamental understanding of the body's energy systems. This somewhat complex science of energy systems is explained in detail as follows.

Energy Systems

The energy released from the food you consume is utilized to manufacture a chemical compound called adenosine triphosphate or ATP. Muscle action is powered by the energy yielded from the hydrolysis of this compound. ATP can be produced by three pathways: two are considered anaerobic (without oxygen), the other aerobic (with oxygen).

The first pathway is called ATP-PC (phosphocreatine). PC, similar to ATP, is stored in the muscle and has an extremely high-energy yield. The PC system itself is anaerobic, and the total amount of ATP that can be produced through this mechanism is finite. The ATP-PC pathway becomes involved when muscles are giving maximal effort, such as pitching a fastball or sprinting 20 feet after a fly ball. The energy reserves from this system are appropriately 10 to 15 seconds.

The second pathway capable of producing ATP is termed anaerobic glycolysis—frequently referred to as the lactic acid system. This system, as the name suggests, is anaerobic and does not involve oxygen. During glycolysis, carbohydrates (glycogen or glucose) are broken down to form ATP.

Anaerobic glycolysis takes over where the ATP-PC system leaves off, allowing you to extend high-intensity exercise. However, the buildup of lactic acid (lactate) triggers the commencement of fatigue (and the slowing of anaerobic glycolysis), usually, depending on the individual, within two-and-one-half minutes or so after the start of vigorous work. In essence, the process forces you to discontinue exercising, or at least lower the intensity considerably to facilitate the removal of lactic acid from the body. Examples where this system comes into play include sprinting 400 meters or swimming as hard as possible for two minutes.

The final pathway in the energy production chain is the aerobic system. This system supplies the body with long-term energy and involves the use of oxygen. After two-and-a-half to three minutes of exercise, the body's ATP requirements are met mostly by the aerobic system. Unlike glycolysis, which can only use carbohydrates to free energy, the aerobic metabolism is able to break down both fats and proteins along with carbohydrates to produce ATP. Some popular forms of aerobic exercise include long distance cycling, running, and rowing.

It is important to note that the transition between energy pathways is not an instantaneous change, but instead a gradual shift from one system to another. For example, when jumping rope all-out for 30 seconds, energy comes from a combination of the ATP-PC and lactic acid systems. In another example, the energy for sprinting 800 meters would come from both anaerobic pathways and the aerobic system. Table 4-1 gives an example of the energy pathway continuum.

```
ATP-PC >>>>>>>>>Anaerobic Glycolysis>>>>>>>>>>Aerobic System

Time:    15 seconds>    2 minutes>    4 minutes>    30 minutes>
```

Table 4-1. Energy pathway continuum

Physical Fitness for Softball

Softball is a sport punctuated with short, explosive bursts of speed and power. Therefore, the demands of the game are mostly anaerobic. More specifically the ATP-PC system takes precedence, since the average movement by a softball player during competition lasts only a few seconds.

While short-duration, explosive activities such as swinging a bat and lunging for a line drive are most common on the softball field, conditioning your body to play the game does not just consist of ATP-PC type training. Softball conditioning entails a gradual build-up of your fitness level and requires all of the following: a solid aerobic base, a highly conditioned lactic acid system, and, finally, a fine-tuned ATP-PC system. How you will attain this balanced conditioning will be discussed in detail in Chapter 5.

Modes of Softball Conditioning

Due to the popularity of physical conditioning throughout the athletic community in recent years, an almost endless number of options are at your disposal when it comes to training your energy systems. Presented next are some of the most popular and effective.

Running

Running is covered first in this section because, simply stated, it works. Running is, in the opinion of most sports-training specialists, the best form of conditioning for explosive sport athletes. After all, explosive sports, including softball, are performed on your feet, so it stands to reason that a training method where you move from place to place in an erect position would be most desirable.

In addition to the phenomenal physical-conditioning qualities, running also yields positive psychological effects. Traversing along a picturesque beach or scenic path does wonders for your state of mind. And it makes no difference whether you're training your anaerobic system with sets of explosive 10-yards sprints or your aerobic metabolism with a slow-paced five-mile jog. The results to your mind-set are the same.

As with all exercise modalities, running is not without its drawbacks. Most notable, it is hard on the knees, feet, shins, and lower back, as the constant pounding of footfall after footfall takes its toll on the body. This can be alleviated to some extent by keeping the majority of your running workouts to soft surfaces such as rubberized running tracks, turf fields, and low-cut grass. Treadmills also provide a soft surface on which to run, but working out on them tends to be less effective than moving your body on solid ground.

If you do, as suggested, make running an integral part of your softball-conditioning program, you'll have to take some precautions. This is especially true if you have a history of impact related injuries. The following are some helpful tips to keep you running injury free:

• *Use proper footwear*: It is imperative that you have running shoes that fit, are comfortable, and, most important, are not worn out. It's amazing how many competitive athletes allow their running footwear to deteriorate to the point where training with them becomes downright dangerous. A variety of injuries including ankle sprains, knee twists, and stress fractures could often-times be avoided by simply keeping your running shoes up to date. It is recommended that you maintain two or even three pairs of running footwear at all times, rotating them every third workout or so. When they show any signs of wearing out, replace them immediately. This approach may get somewhat expensive, but it will be well worth the price in terms of preventing injury.

- *Build up gradually*: All running programs should be taken on gradually. Advancing too fast before you're ready increases the risk of injury substantially. Most injuries, whether sustained on the softball diamond or running track, occur when the body is tired. Getting ahead of yourself with your running regime will put your body in a constant state of fatigue, thus increasing the risk of injury. Following the conditioning programs in *Peak Conditioning Training for Softball* will ensure that you progress optimally and safely with your running program.

- *Keep to soft surfaces*: This topic was covered before, but it's important to re-emphasize the point of taking the majority of your running workouts on soft surfaces. Regular running on pavement, blacktop, or even old cinder tracks will eventually lead to injury for most athletes. It may take a little more time to head down to the track, field, beach, or gym than to just open up your front door and hit the streets, but the benefit of enduring a little inconvenience is well worth the consequences of possible injury.

- *Awareness of minor discomforts*: Most experienced runners develop an instinctive feel for when slight discomforts have the potential to become problematic injuries. For instance, when a minor sensation in the front of the lower leg may be the precursor to a debilitating case of shin splints. If you plan to make running a major part of your training regime, you too must develop this intuitive feel for oncoming injuries and then act accordingly. Acting accordingly may entail discontinuing a particular run, switching to a less taxing conditioning method (i.e., stationary biking or swimming), or seeking treatment in the training room.

- *Stretch before and after*: Why you should stretch before and after all workouts and competitions has previously been discussed in detail in this book. Nowhere is this habit more important than when it relates to running workouts. The constant movement and foot pounding makes stretching an important prerequisite for all running softball players.

Stationary Biking

Riding a stationary bike has long been a popular form of exercise for athletes and non-athletes alike. It requires very little in the way of expertise, is a low-impact activity, and offers a method of exercising that can be easily regulated. With the exception of swimming or pool workouts, it is also the most accepted activity prescribed for injured athletes and for competitors returning from long lay-offs.

The key factor to successful stationary bike workouts lies in sustaining your target heart rate. Where running and swimming, for instance, tend to elevate the heart rate to appropriate levels without much conscious effort, stationary biking requires full concentration in order to maintain a target heart rate (target heart rates are discussed in the following chapter). Because of this, it is recommended that you incorporate a heart rate monitor during all stationary bike sessions.

Two popular activities some engage in while riding a stationary bike are reading and watching television. Both are discouraged for serious athletes. Although convenient and time-passing endeavors, they tend to take your attention away form the task at hand, which is, of course, garnering the most productive conditioning workout possible.

Numerous types of stationary bikes are available for your use. They run the gamut from fancy, computerized models that gauge just about everything (i.e., heart rate, calories burned, revolutions per minute, miles traveled, etc.) to the simple hand-operated original gathering dust in your attic or basement. Computerized stationary bikes are preferred by most, but all styles can be utilized for effective workouts. Just make sure the bike is comfortable; has an easily adjustable seat; has durable pedals, preferably ones with foot straps where you can lock in your feet; and has smoothly calibrated tension.

One variation of the stationary bike is worth special mention: the recumbent bike. This equipment provides back support and the pedals are positioned straight in front of you rather than directly below. It is widely used at health and fitness clubs, as well as in many home gyms Athletes with back and neck problems may find the recumbent bike more comfortable than the conventional version.

Elliptical/Cross Trainer

The basic idea behind the development of the elliptical/cross trainer was to simulate the running motion minus the inherent pounding. To a large extent, the designers succeeded. More so than any other fitness equipment available today, the elliptical/cross trainer does in fact mimic running. In addition, it exercises both the lower and upper body in unison, thus promoting a high-level conditioning workout. Unlike many upper/lower body action machines (i.e., cross country ski machines), the elliptical/cross trainer is also easy to operate.

Elliptical/cross trainers are extremely popular and well-represented at commercial health and fitness clubs. They are available for the home but tend to be somewhat pricey, not to mention cumbersome. Overall, these apparatuses rate highly when compared to most fitness conditioning equipment and can be incorporated periodically for those softball players who have the opportunity and inclination. Be aware, however, that while elliptical/cross trainers do simulate running to a large extent, they should not be used as a full-time substitute for hitting the path, track, or beach. As mentioned before, running is far and away the best conditioning vehicle for the competitive softball player and should be employed for the lion's share of your training workouts.

Swimming

Regardless of your proficiency as a swimmer, hitting the pool for a workout has many benefits. Swimming furnishes a fantastic full-body workout, as virtually every muscle in the arms, legs, and torso are involved to some degree. Swimming also provides terrific anaerobic and aerobic benefits and contributes to loosening and toning the muscles of the upper body. (Many top athletes from a variety of sports loosen up in the pool after strenuous upper body strength workouts.) And, the best news of all for softball players concerning water training is that swimming is extremely easy on the joints and body in general, offering perhaps the ultimate low-impact workout. (How many competitive swimmers do you know who've lost time in the pool due to injury?) Because of this, pool workouts are universally recognized as the most efficient way for injured athletes to maintain their conditioning during competitive downtime. Most major college sports programs have specially designed water-training protocols for their injured athletes to follow.

If your swimming skills are like most softball players and leave something to be desired, don't knock water workouts off your training agenda just yet; a plethora of accessories are available, from kick boards to specially designed flotation vests that will help you keep your head above water as you get your exercise. So if you have access to the appropriate facilities, give your body a well-deserved break from the pounding of other forms of training and jump in the pool for a workout.

Rowing

World-class rowers are known for their high levels of physical conditioning. They consistently score high on all varieties of cardiovascular fitness tests, and their training regimes are viewed by many in the sports conditioning community as the most demanding in all of competitive sports.

For most of you, rowing will be accomplished indoors on a rowing machine. While rowing on a lake or river is extremely pleasant and exhilarating, it does require expertise that most softball players just don't have. However, if you do live near a body of water appropriate for rowing and are willing to put in the requisite time to learn, by all means rent or buy yourself a scull, and go to it.

Performed indoors or outdoors, rowing is an extraordinary form of exercise, one that will train both your aerobic and anaerobic systems completely, while at the same time building up the muscles of your back, shoulders, biceps, and forearms. Additionally, indoor rowing on a rowing machine is very easy to learn.

The only down side to rowing is it can be somewhat taxing on the lower back. The repetitive motion of leaning forward and then back causes strain to that area. Therefore, if you have a history of back problems, rowing may not be for you.

The two standard types of rowing machines are flywheel and hydraulic cylinder rowers. Both machines are adequate; however, many fitness professionals prefer the flywheel model because it more closely simulates water rowing and places slightly less stress on the lower back.

Stair Climbing

Once on the cutting age of the fitness boom, stair climbing fell out of favor with the health club set a decade or so ago. In recent years, however, the training option has made a comeback, and rows of stair climbing machines can be seen at most health and fitness clubs around the country today.

In order to get the most out of your stair climbing workouts, incorporating proper technique is essential. Many athletes make the mistake of using the handlebars for support during execution, either by grabbing them with their hands or leaning over them and bracing themselves on their elbows. Both actions undermine the effectiveness and intensity of the exercise. As such, make sure when training on a stair climber to only use the handlebars to maintain balance and not to support your body weight.

Although the newer stair climbers are much better designed than in the past, some athletes still complain of knee and hip pain after climbing workouts. This complaint is due to slight hyperextension of the knee joint and repetitive hip motion. If you experience any pain, stair climbing should be avoided.

5

Year-Round Softball Conditioning

As mentioned in the previous chapter, in order to ready your body to play peak performance softball, you must condition all three energy systems thoroughly. This year-round endeavor will include four separate phases: aerobic base, lactic acid, ATP-PC, and maintenance. After the parameters of aerobic and anaerobic training are set forth, all four phases will be discussed in detail.

Aerobic Training

Aerobic training is usually defined as any reasonably low-intensity activity that is sustained for an extended period of time. Although some fitness professionals feel aerobic benefits can be achieved in as little as 12 continuous minutes of training, for softball purposes it is best to work within 20-minute to 45-minute time parameters.

In addition to workout duration, the intensity at which you exercise must be taken into account. The simplest way to measure the intensity of an aerobic activity is by using percentages of your maximal heart rate (max HR). Your estimated max HR can be easily figured by subtracting your age from 220. An 18-year-old softball player, for example, would have a max HR of 202 (220-18 = 202). After determining your max HR, you can then find your suggested aerobic training range. Most experts agree that to acquire aerobic benefits, you should train somewhere between 75 and 85 percent of your max HR. Using the previous example, 18-year-old athletes would be required to elevate their heart rates between 151 to 172 beats per minute (bpm) to achieve satisfactory aerobic conditioning benefits. Of course, much depends upon the duration of the activity, the particular mode of aerobic exercise being used, and the genetic capacity of the individual.

Your heart rate can be conveniently calculated with the help of a heart rate monitor. These devices can be purchased at most sporting goods stores and through fitness equipment catalogs. Some specialized aerobic training equipment also have built in heart rate monitors. If a heart rate monitor is not available to you, simply determine your heart rate by pinpointing your radial artery in your wrist and count the beats per minute.

Softball and Aerobic Training

Aerobic training has gone through a number of public relations transformations over the years. When it first became popular in the early 1970s, it was hailed as perhaps the quintessential fitness tool, favored by both athletes and the general public for its conditioning benefits and health promoting qualities.

In recent years, however, the attitude toward aerobic training has shifted considerably, especially among those in the sports-training community. While the proven health benefits of enhanced cardio respiratory function, elevated HDL cholesterol (the good cholesterol), and lower blood pressure are not disputed, engaging in excessive amounts of aerobic training has shown to be somewhat problematic for explosive sport athletes like softball players. Some negative byproducts include inhibiting explosiveness, contributing to the loss of hard-earned muscle mass, and increasing susceptibility to impact and overtraining related injuries.

Now, before you swear off aerobic workouts forever, keep in mind that while this type of training is not the fitness panacea it was once thought to be, neither is it a worthless conditioning method that will ruin your softball game. The truth is that aerobic exercise, if employed properly and in reasonable moderation, can be a useful component of a softball player's overall conditioning program. The following are just a few reasons why:

• *Provides a conditioning base*: In order to prepare your body for intense anaerobic, softball-specific workouts, you must first develop a solid conditioning base. Consistent aerobic training in the early off-season will provide this. In essence, aerobic training sets the stage for subsequent anaerobic workouts. Those athletes who attempt to jump right into high intensity anaerobic training sessions without any preconditioning are setting themselves up for failure, not to mention injury.

• *Improves recovery time*: Any softball player who finds herself winded after beating out an infield hit is in sub par aerobic condition. Achieving a high degree of aerobic fitness will enhance your ability to recover between plays, games, and workouts. The increased flow of oxygen to your lungs improves short-term recovery and assists in the removal of lactic acid from the system, a key factor in long-term recuperation.

• *Weight control*: Aerobic exercise speeds up the metabolism, transforming the body into a virtual fat-burning furnace. If you have a tendency to put on unwanted weight, regular aerobic workouts combined with a low-calorie diet will counteract this condition.

While it's not recommended for softball players to engage in aerobic training during the regular season, if excess weight is hindering your performance, exceptions can be made.

- *Maintains conditioning during down time*: At times over the course of your training year, participating in fast-paced, high-intensity activities like plyometrics or speed training will not be an option—for instance, when recovering from a lower leg injury. In this case and others, non-impact aerobic training, such as stationary biking, swimming, or rowing, can be incorporated to maintain adequate levels of physical conditioning until you're ready for more demanding workouts.

- *Perform better late*: Being in aerobic shape will allow you to perform at peak levels in the late innings of a game and toward the later stages of the competitive campaign. Athletes who are strong and productive in late-game and season situations are usually the ones who've conditioned their aerobic systems diligently.

Anaerobic Training

Physical activity is considered anaerobic when you are exercising at about 85 to 100 percent of your maximum heart rate. The following instances are examples of when softball players work anaerobically during competition: sprinting from first to third on a base hit to right field, pitching a fastball, and rising up explosively out of a catchers stance to throw out a potential base stealer.

The key ingredient to successful anaerobic workouts is intensity. You must work as hard as possible for the prescribed time and/or distance. As discussed previously, the high-effort nature of anaerobic training will allow you to exercise only in short bouts, two-and-a-half minutes being the maximum for even highly conditioned, world-class athletes, before fatigue gets the best of you. Although some suggest that you should monitor your heart rate during anaerobic workouts, it is not always necessary, as the pain in your lungs and legs should let you know in no uncertain terms that you're in your "anaerobic training zone."

Softball and Anaerobic Conditioning

As mentioned earlier, softball is an anaerobic sport. Softball players should fully condition their entire anaerobic system, both lactic acid and ATP-PC, in an organized and progressive manner. Doing so will ensure that you achieve peak performance levels on the softball field.

Work:Rest Ratios

When designing anaerobic conditioning programs for softball, it is necessary to incorporate specific work:rest ratios. The work:rest ratio denotes the work or exercise period of an activity relative to the rest interval. For example, if you were to sprint for 25 seconds and then rest for 50 seconds before sprinting again, the work:rest ratio would be 1:2. This type of organized training will produce optimal benefits in your anaerobic conditioning.

Typically, the longer the bout of anaerobic activity, the smaller the work:rest ratio. For instance, jumping rope all-out for two minutes would require a work:rest ratio of approximately 1:1. At the other end of the spectrum, sprinting up a steep grade hill for 15 seconds would call for a work:rest ratio of approximately 1:3. Table 5-1 summarizes the various durations of anaerobic training and their appropriate work:rest ratios.

Work/Time in Seconds	Work:Rest Ratios
0 to 45	1:3
45 to 120	1:2 to 1:1
120 to 150	1:1

Table 5-1. Anaerobic exercise times and approximate work:rest ratios

Year-Round Conditioning Program for Softball

Your softball-conditioning schedule will consist of four separate phases: base, lactic acid, softball specific/ATP-PC, and maintenance. The first three phases will contribute toward progressively building your level of conditioning. The final phase, as the name suggests, will concentrate on maintaining the high degree of fitness you've developed. Following, all four phases are explained in detail. At the conclusion of each explanation, sample training schedules are presented.

Phase 1

Duration: 8 weeks

Workouts Per Week: 2 to 4

Description: Phase 1 will begin in the early off-season about a month or so after the conclusion of your season. The focus will be on gradually developing an aerobic conditioning base. The training sessions will range between 20 and 40 minutes in duration. Over the last two weeks of this phase, transition workouts will be implemented where aerobic training will be combined with low-intensity anaerobic work. Table 5-2 presents a sample Phase 1 training schedule.

Week 1:	Monday	20 minutes	Friday	22 minutes
Week 2:	Sunday Tuesday	24 minutes 25 minutes	Friday	26 minutes
Week 3:	Sunday Tuesday	28 minutes 30 minutes	Friday	30 minutes
Week 4:	Sunday Tuesday	32 minutes 34 minutes	Saturday	34 minutes
Week 5:	Monday Wednesday	35 minutes 36 minutes	Thursday Saturday	36 minutes 38 minutes
Week 6:	Monday Tuesday	40 minutes 40 minutes	Thursday Saturday	40 minutes 40 minutes
Week 7:	Tuesday Friday	35 minutes/low-intensity anaerobic workout 30 minutes/low-intensity anaerobic workout		
Week 8:	Tuesday Friday	30 minutes/low-intensity anaerobic workout 30 minutes/low-intensity anaerobic workout		

Table 5-2. Sample eight-week aerobic conditioning program

Phase 2

Duration: 10 weeks

Workouts Per Week: 2 to 3

Description: Phase 2 marks the beginning of the anaerobic part of your conditioning program. The concentration will be on training the lactic acid system. For softball purposes, 30 to 90 second bouts of exercise will be incorporated. Because of the intensity of this type of training, no more than two to three weekly workouts are suggested.

Be advised that lactic acid training is by far the most challenging (and painful) phase of your year-round conditioning program. It will tax both your body and heart in equal measure. But by persevering through this demanding phase, you'll be taking a major step toward achieving the best physical condition of your life. Table 5-3 presents a sample Phase 2 training schedule.

Week	Sets per Workout	Exercise Duration	Rest
#1	4	90 seconds	2.75 minutes
#2	5	75 seconds	2.5 minutes
#3	6	60 seconds	2.25 minutes
#4	6	60 seconds	2 minutes
#5	7	50 seconds	1.75 minutes
#6	7	50 seconds	1.5 minutes
#7	7	45 seconds	1.5 minutes
#8	8	45 seconds	1.5 minutes
#9	9	30 seconds	1.25 minutes
#10	9	30 seconds	1.25 minutes

Table 5.3. Sample Phase 2 training schedule

Phase 3

Duration: 8 weeks

Workouts Per Week: 2 to 3

Description: This final off-season phase is designed to bring you to optimal softball shape. The training will consist of short-duration bouts of exercise similar to what you'd be required to do on the softball field. Conditioning your ATP-PC system will be the priority of Phase 3.

The first two weeks of Phase 3 will involve transition workouts combining both lactic acid and ATP-PC training. The final six weeks of this phase will focus exclusively on ATP-PC training. This training can be accomplished by incorporating a variety of methods including uphill running, plyometric exercise, or agility training, all of which you'll read about later in the book. Table 5-4 presents a sample Phase 3 training schedule.

Phase 4

Duration: Entire competitive season

Workouts per week: 2 to 3

Description: Maintaining a high level of physical conditioning throughout the competitive campaign is absolutely necessary if you hope to play peak performance softball. It is also no easy task. Unlike movement oriented sports such as field hockey, basketball, and lacrosse, where participating in the games and scrimmages provide

Week	Sets per Workout	Exercise Duration	Rest
#1	10	30 seconds	1.25 minutes
#2	10	30 seconds	70 seconds
#3	12	20 seconds	65 seconds
#4	12	20 seconds	60 seconds
#5	14	15 seconds	45 seconds
#6	16	15 seconds	40 seconds
#7	20	10 seconds	30 seconds
#8	20	10 seconds	30 seconds

Table 5.4. Sample Phase 3 training schedule

solid conditioning workouts, competing on the softball diamond contributes very little to your overall conditioning. Therefore, softball players must be diligent during the regular season in running outfield sprints, performing agility drills, and working out on a variety of fitness equipment.

Your in-season conditioning workouts will focus on repetitive short to medium duration bouts of exercise (10 to 45 seconds), with only periodic aerobic training sessions—aerobic fitness tends to be maintained by doing regular anaerobic exercise. The workouts will take place either before or after games and during practice sessions on non-game days. Table 5-5 presents two sample weeks of Phase 4 in-season conditioning training.

Week #1	Week #2
Monday 4 x 200-yard sprints 4 x 30 seconds of jumping rope 6 x 15 seconds of lateral line hops	**Monday** 5 x 45-second stationary bike intervals 6 x 15 seconds of lateral slides 20 minutes of jogging
Wednesday 4 x 80-yard sprints 6 x 40-yard sprints 30 minutes of stationary biking	**Thursday** 4 x 100-yard sprints 4 x 40-yard sprints 6 x 20-yard sprints
Friday 4 x 40-yard uphill sprints 4 x 20-yard towing sprints 6 x 15 seconds of rim touches	

Table 5.5. Sample Phase 4 training schedule

6

Conditioning for Recreational Softball Players

After reading the previous five chapters of *Peak Conditioning Training for Softball*, you've surely noticed that the focus is on the competitive athlete. However, any book devoted to softball improvement would not be complete without at least some attention given to recreational softball players. Chapter 6 is for the thousands upon thousands of individuals who participate annually in recreational softball leagues. This chapter's concentration is on manageability, with time, age, and athletic ability of the player taken into consideration. Recreational conditioning program parameters are discussed, complete with training modality explanations, sample workouts, weekly conditioning schedules, and recreational athlete specific training tips.

Program Parameters

Recreational softball players are best served following a three-pronged approach to conditioning, which includes strength, aerobic, and explosiveness training. The objective is to accomplish two of each type of workout over a seven-day period. The warm-up, cool-down, and flexibility training protocols that were detailed in Chapter 1 will precede and follow each bout of training. The workout sessions themselves, which should be incorporated on a year-round basis, will take place on either a four or five day-per-week schedule.

Please note that before beginning this program, it is imperative that you become familiar with the information put forth in *Peak Conditioning Training for Softball*. Reading through the entire book before commencing will ensure that your training will be safe and productive.

Explosiveness Training

Recreational athlete's explosiveness training will consist of balance exercises, agility drills, and anaerobic interval work. All three of these training disciplines should be performed in the same workout. The following sequence within the workout is suggested: balance, agility, anaerobic. This order allows you to gradually build in intensity as the workout progresses. Many recreational softball players execute explosiveness workouts prior to games or practices, feeling it provides a terrific warm-up for competition.

Sample Explosiveness Workout

- One Leg Stands: 3 sets on each leg held for 40 seconds
- Line Touches: 3 sets on each leg for 12 repetitions
- Front Line Hops: 3 sets, 15 to 20 seconds each
- Side Line Hops: 3 sets, 15 to 20 seconds each
- 2 x 80 Yard Sprint*
- 4 x 40 Yard Sprint*
- 6 x 20 Yard Sprint*

* Incorporate work/rest ratios detailed in Chapter 5.

Strength Training

Both of your weekly strength workouts will entail a full-body workout. As is the case for competitive athletes, multi-joint lifts (movements that exercise more than one muscle group) will be the focus of your strength program. Muscle groups should always be exercised from largest to smallest within the workout (hips, legs, upper back, and so on down the line). More ambitious recreational athletes may want to include an extra strength workout to their training week. Should this be the case, splitting your routine between upper body and lower body/core training is suggested.

Sample Strength Workout

- Squat: 4 sets, 12 to 20 repetitions
- Leg Curl: 3 sets, 15 repetitions
- Pull-Down: 3 sets, 12 repetitions
- Incline Press: 3 sets, 12 repetitions
- Floor Back Raise: 3 sets, 20 repetitions
- Bench Crunch: 4 sets, 25 repetitions
- Upright Row: 3 sets, 12 repetitions

Aerobic Training

Your biweekly aerobic sessions will require that you closely follow the training parameters discussed in Chapter 5. It is especially important during these workouts to maintain a target heart rate within your "aerobic training range" (70 to 85 percent of your maximal heart rate). Not doing so will be a waste of your time and energy. Any of the exercise modalities (stationary biking, swimming, rowing, etc.) detailed in Chapter 4 may be used for aerobic training. However, as is the case for your competitive counterparts, running is the preferred form of conditioning for softball players. Depending on your level of fitness, aerobic workouts for recreational athletes will last between 18 and 30 minutes.

Four-Day Conditioning Schedule

Monday:	Aerobic training (morning) and strength training (evening)
Tuesday:	Balance/agility/anaerobic training
Wednesday:	Off
Thursday:	Aerobic training
Friday: (evening)	Balance/agility/anaerobic training (morning) and strength training
Saturday:	Off
Sunday:	Off

Five-Day Conditioning Schedule

Monday:	Aerobic training
Tuesday:	Strength training
Wednesday:	Off
Thursday:	Balance/agility/anaerobic
Friday:	Aerobic training
Saturday:	Off
Sunday: (evening)	Strength training (morning) and balance/agility/anaerobic training

Conditioning Tips for Recreational Athletes

Take Five

In this case, taking five doesn't refer to enjoying a five-minute break from the rigors of a workout. It actually means taking five consecutive weeks to really focus on developing a solid base of strength and conditioning. This approach will pay great dividends for the recreational athlete, because once a strong base of shape is achieved, maintaining conditioning throughout a busy year is much easier. The occasional missed workout or minor injury won't set you back to any great extent once you've acquired a base of strength and fitness. Plus, the likelihood of sustaining a serious training related injury will be considerably less likely when you're in shape. Base building is best incorporated early in the off-season, approximately six months before the start of league play. Some more dedicated types may want to consider attending a fitness camp or workout spa to get off on the right foot conditioning wise. These camps/spas usually run for about two weeks and provide a plethora of fitness options, along with featuring experienced staff to guide you through your workouts. Fitness camps/spas are regularly advertised in fitness magazines and on the Internet.

Organize, Organize, Organize

Competitive athletes are usually afforded the luxury of having coaches, trainers, and more experienced teammates help them plan and regulate their workout schedules. Recreational players will enjoy no such luxury. Basically, unless you engage a full-time trainer, you'll be on your own when it comes to organizing your conditioning program. One proven organizing strategy you may want to try is at the beginning of each training week pencil in on a calendar exactly when you'll be training, where the session will take place, and what will be accomplished during the workout. While you may not be able to follow your penciled schedule to the letter, this approach will give you a framework from which to work.

A Little Is Better than Nothing

Because of time constraints, many recreational athletes will be hard pressed to follow the previously referenced conditioning program on a weekly basis. In this case, it is important to remember that a little training is better than none at all. Even adhering to an abbreviated routine is enough to improve your softball performance and provide general health and fitness benefits.

Use the Upcoming Softball Season as Motivation

In most parts of the country recreational softball leagues begin in the mid-spring and run through the summer months. The fall and winter leave most non-competitive softball players idle as far as game play is concerned. This is a terrific opportunity to improve your strength and conditioning, using the approaching league season as a motivator to attaining top shape. The goal, similar to that of full-time athletes, is to slowly build up your fitness level over the off-season for peaking at the start of league play.

Workout with a Teammate

If you happen to have an equally dedicated softball teammate who is interested in working out with you, by all means, take him or her up on it. A training partner will provide a spotter in the weight room, a motivator to boost your efforts, and, perhaps most important, a presence to ensure that you show up for scheduled workouts consistently and in a timely manner. (If you know that your teammate will be at the track, gym, or field at a specific time, you're much more likely not to blow off the workout or arrive late.)

So call around to your teammates and float the idea of softball conditioning workouts. If you find no takers, feel free to approach other workout-minded friends or acquaintances, as training with a partner, even if it's not another softball player, is well worth it.

Consider a Personal Trainer

Personal trainers have become very popular in recent years among both competitive and recreational athletes. Some professional athletes actually employ full-time trainers that travel with them from city to city throughout the year. Taking on a personal fitness trainer may be a route you want to explore. However, working out with a trainer has advantages and disadvantages.

Advantages

- Help with conditioning program organization.

- Teach and monitor proper exercise execution.

- Provide motivation and support during workouts.

- Act as spotters during the execution of heavy lifts.

- Help you negotiate through a crowded public gym—which comes in extremely handy if you train at peak hours (weekdays from 5:30 PM to 8:30 PM).

Disadvantages

- Cost. Some trainers charge $100 per hour or more.

- Availability. Since you're most likely not your trainer's only client, the timing of workouts may not always fit neatly into your schedule.

- Overreliability. Becoming overly reliant on your personnel trainer will hinder your ability to experience quality workouts on your own.

- Qualifications. Unfortunately, a small number of personal trainers are not up to the task. It is your responsibility to carefully screen and analyze prospective trainers. If the one you choose doesn't suit your needs and expectations, feel free to move on to another. After all, your money and time are extremely important.

Take Advantage of Impromptu Workouts

Impromptu workouts are simply workouts that you didn't expect to have. A cancellation of a lunchtime business meeting, delayed travel plans, a bout of insomnia are all occasions for impromptu workouts. As mentioned previously, competitive athletes have much of their workout schedule laid out for them. Recreational participants, on the other hand, must scrap and fight to keep current with their conditioning programs. Taking advantage of impromptu sessions when they present themselves is one way to do this.

PART III
STRENGTH TRAINING FOR SOFTBALL

7

Softball Strength Training Basics and Principles

Saying that strength training for sports has come a long way in recent years would be an understatement. Not too long ago, strength work was strongly frowned upon in the athletic community. The thought was that the weight room was a place for bodybuilders, power lifters, and Olympic weight lifters, not for conventional team sport athletes, many of whom relied on speed and skill to succeed.

Eventually, athletes who participated in pure strength sports, such as football, wrestling, and shot putting, began to test the strength training waters. Their experiences, to the surprise of many, was extremely positive. Not only did strength and power improve for these individuals, but performance in their respective sports did as well.

With the genie out of the bottle, so to speak, skill sport athletes, such as basketball, tennis, and soccer players, got into the strength training act. Female athletes, including many top softball players, also began to pump iron on a regular basis. Today strength training is not only accepted throughout the sports world, but recognized as an absolute necessity for athletes dedicated to reaching their full potential.

Why Strength Train for Softball

Strength training provides many by-products that enhance performance on the softball field. For example, you will improve your ability to hit with power and throw with velocity, as increases in overall body strength allow you to generate more force during the performance of these activities. Your speed and quickness will increase substantially, especially those crucial first few steps out of the batters box or in pursuit of a sinking line drive in the outfield. Most fast and explosive runners are strong and well muscled. If you don't believe this just take one look at world-class sprinters such as Gail Devers and Marion Jones. Stamina and endurance will be much enhanced through your weight room workouts as well, allowing you to perform efficiently at the tail end of a double-header or at the end of a long, grueling softball season.

Training with weights has been proven to be your best defense against injury. Stronger muscles will help you withstand the rigors of intense practice sessions and exhausting conditioning workouts. If you do happen to sustain an injury, strength training will be an integral and helpful part of the rehabilitation protocol. Additional muscle mass will also improve your ability to absorb contact, so those collisions at home plate or at second base will be less taxing on the body. Also, as a direct result of lifting weights and becoming stronger and more powerful, your confidence in yourself and your softball game will increase dramatically. As anyone involved in competitive sports knows, without confidence your chances of success are nil.

Strength training promotes team camaraderie as well. The weight room or team training facility is a sanctuary where athletes can workout in a congenial and positive energy environment, away from the critical eye of coaches. Teammates can encourage each other to give their best efforts. In the process, they'll become closer as a ball club, which is a key ingredient to a winning team. Furthermore, if your goal is to add lean body weight to your frame, combining strength training with a healthy high-calorie diet is the ticket. Conversely, if losing weight will help your performance in-between the lines, training with weights and building additional muscle increases the metabolic rate, an important factor in burning fat more efficiently. While you will achieve plenty of other benefits by strength training, the aforementioned reasons should be more than enough to convince you to hit the weights.

Before moving on, one aspect of strength training of particular concern to female athletes should be discussed: the common fear that lifting weights regularly will increase an athlete's muscularity to the point where the "feminine look" is diminished or lost. This worry is erroneous. The fact is that it is extremely difficult, if not impossible, for women, because of their genetic make-up, to build large amounts of muscle mass naturally (without the use of muscle enhancing substances such as anabolic steroids). Strength training correctly has shown to not only improve sports performance but to produce strong, toned, and attractive bodies in both men and women.

Strength Training Basics

Before beginning your strength training program, you must first become familiar with the basic aspects of working out with weights. The following information will help you get started on the right track.

Weight Training Equipment

You will be using three basic types of weight training equipment during your strength workouts: free weights (accompanied by a variety of exercise benches and power racks), a selection of weight machines, and medicine balls of various weights. Most gyms and team-training facilities have a full complement of each. Free weights consist of barbells and dumbbells. A good exercise bench should be sturdy and easily adjustable, allowing for different incline positions. Power racks are used for squatting and other heavy standing movements (i.e., hang cleans, push presses, high pulls, etc.) A substantial number of strength training machines are available for your use. The most useful include the lat machine, leg press, cable row, leg extension, leg curl, and pullover machine. Medicine balls are weighted spheres that come in an assortment of weights, sizes, and colors. Rubber medicine balls are recommended because they grip easily, bounce evenly when they hit the floor, and are generally safer to use.

Attire

- *Clothing*: Loose, comfortable fitting clothing is best for weight room workouts. The most important factor is that what you wear does not in any way hinder your movement and exercise performance. In a cold gym, it is suggested that you wear some type of sweat suit, at least until your muscles warm up.

- *Footwear*: Some footwear is specifically designed for weightlifting. However, most basketball or cross training sneakers are suitable. Running or jogging shoes lack lateral support and should not be worn while strength training.

- *Gloves*: Just as many softball players wear batting gloves, many regular weight trainers wear weightlifting gloves. Some feel gloves provide a better grip on barbells and dumbbells, and gloves do help to prevent calluses from developing on your hands.

- *Weightlifting belt*: A weightlifting belt is typically five to eight inches wide and made of leather or nylon. Belts are designed to support the lower back during heavy lifts. Although some trainers and conditioning specialists feel that weight belts are not necessary and that any benefit gained is mostly psychological, wearing one during heavy-standing lifts is still recommended.

- *Straps*: Straps are used mostly by bodybuilders to prevent grip fatigue during exercises, such as chin-ups and upright rows. Softball players have no need to use straps in their strength workouts. In fact, gripping barbells, dumbbells, chinning bars, etc., helps to improve forearm strength, which is an attribute all softball players covet.

- *Waist harness*: A waist harness allows you to add weight to your frame when performing exercises like dips and chin-ups.

Safety

Injuries in the weight room occur frequently and can be serious. That said, many injuries could be avoided by taking some simple precautions. The most important are as follows:

- *Warm-up*: If you hope to reduce your chances of suffering a strength training related injury, you must be sufficiently warmed up before each and every weight workout. Refer to Chapter 1 for information on warming up.

- *Use spotters*: Without exception, it is essential that an experienced spotter be incorporated when you are performing heavy sets of bench presses, incline presses, shoulder presses, and squats. Neglecting this advice can result in serious injury. In addition to ensuring safety, an attentive, knowledgeable spotter can correct errors in lifting form and help you get the most out of a set by giving just enough assistance to enable you to complete that final, strength promoting repetition.

- *Heavy singles*: Many strength training-induced injuries would be prevented if one-repetition maximum lifts were avoided. Besides trying to impress your friends in the gym, absolutely no reason exists to perform heavy singles. Three to four repetition sets are far superior to maximum-weight single lifts for building strength, power, and muscle.

- *Collars*: You should get in the habit of using collars for all barbell lifts. Collars ensure that weight plates do not slide and cause you to lose control of the bar.

- *Check equipment*: All equipment should be checked for safety before use. For example, make sure that benches are sturdy, plates are tight to the bar, machine cables are not worn, and all collars are secure.

- Be aware: It is important that you are aware of what's going on around you in the weight room. Awareness is especially important when training in a crowded facility. Although you may be following all the proper weight training protocol, other exercisers may not be, so keep your eyes open to prevent a mishap.

Weight Room Etiquette

If you're going to be a regular in the weight room, which you will be if your coaches have anything to say about it, learning proper gym etiquette is imperative. Following the simple rules of weight room conduct will go a long way toward making your (and others) strength training experience a productive, safe, and pleasant one.

- *Abstain from horseplay*: Fooling around during your strength sessions will not only hinder your progress, it can be downright dangerous to you and those around you. So do yourself and everybody else in the gym a favor, save the horseplay for after the workout.

- *Replace all weights after use*: If you've ever been in a gym or weight room where weight plates were scattered about, machine pins missing, and dumbbells placed in the non-weight appropriate racks, you know how unpleasant this workout environment can be. It is imperative that you replace all weights, bars, and any other equipment to their proper place after use. Pay particular attention to returning dumbbells and barbell plates to their designated racks. Most public fitness centers and health clubs have signs posted reminding members to replace all weights after use. Take heed of this advice and replace all equipment after you're finished with it.

- *Let others work in*: If you're working out in a crowded public gym, more often than not someone will want to alternate sets with you on a particular piece of equipment. Although this may be somewhat disruptive to the pace of your workout, proper weight room etiquette calls for you to allow others to work in. Of course, if you're training with a partner, this type of disruption won't be a problem.

- *Wipe down all equipment after use*: Nobody wants to work out on wet, sweaty equipment. So after concluding your sets, be sure to towel down the equipment for the next person.

Strength Training Principles

- *Sets and repetitions*: Sets and repetitions are the units of measure used in strength training. For example, shoulder pressing a pair of dumbbells 12 consecutive times with only a brief pause in-between lifts constitutes one set of 12 repetitions. The simple notation used to indicate such an effort is 1 x 12. The first number listed always represents sets and the second figure represents repetitions.

- *Multi-joint exercises*: Multi-joint exercises work more than one muscle group at a time. An example of a multi-joint lift is the incline press, which exercises a variety of muscle groups, including the upper chest, anterior deltoids, and triceps. These types of movements should be the focal point of your strength training program.

- *Combination exercises*: Combination movements are multi-joint exercises, as they work numerous muscles at once, but they tend to be more complicated to execute and are performed in an explosive manner. Some examples of combination lifts include hang cleans, push presses, high pulls, and explosive squats. These types of exercises are discussed in detail later in the book.

- *Single-joint exercises*: Sometimes referred to as auxiliary exercises, single-joint movements work one muscle group at a time. Two examples of single-joint exercises are barbell curls for the biceps and leg extensions for the quadriceps. These types if exercises will supplement the multi-joint and combination movements in your strength program.

- *Train your largest muscles first*: It is important that you train your muscles from largest to smallest during all strength workouts. Two basic reasons are behind this idea. First, the smaller muscle is already the weak link in the strength chain when executing any multi-joint lift. For example, in the squat, training your lower back with exercises like hyper-extensions or floor back raises before squatting would further weaken the smaller muscle (lower back), thus limiting the workload for the stronger muscle groups (hips and quadriceps). Second, the bigger the body part, the more energy it takes to train. Because your energy levels are obviously higher at the beginning of a workout, it is best to exercise larger muscles (upper back, legs, chest, etc.) first in your weightlifting sessions.

- *Pyramid sets*: For the most effective results from your strength training efforts, incorporating pyramid sets within your workout is recommended. As the term suggests, pyramiding entails progressing from lighter weight sets to your heaviest set, then lowering the resistance on your last few sets. The notation would look something like this: 1 x 15, 1 x 10, 1 x 6, 1 x 8, 1 x 10. Training in this manner will help ensure maximum muscle fatigue and strength gains.

- *Strength progression*: Obviously, the major premise of a sound strength training program is progression. To encourage this, it is best to perform the majority of your sets (not including warm-up sets) near the point of muscular failure. For instance, if your program calls for a 10-repetition set, you would chose a weight that allows you to complete 10 repetitions and no more. When more than 10 repetitions can be executed in good form, it is time to add weight. Usually a five-percent increase is sufficient for multi-joint exercises.

   Of course, finding the appropriate resistance level for each exercise in your program will require a period of trail and error, especially if you're new to strength training or coming from a long lay-off. Keep in mind that strength progression usually comes quickly for beginners. It is not atypical for a novice trainer to make substantial gains in strength and muscle in as little as three months. Unfortunately, as time moves forward and your body becomes accustomed to the rigors of weight training, increases become more difficult. Progression is still possible, however, albeit at a slower pace, and should always remain the priority.

- *Consistency*: If you hope to reach your strength potential, you must be consistent. Consistency may seem a "no brainer" and not worth mentioning, but consistency is so vital to the strength-building process that without it failure is not only possible but assured. You must push yourself to get to the gym or training facility regularly and then proceed to work hard when you get there. Even missing a few scheduled workouts can set you back substantially. Lifting weights, perhaps more so than any other conditioning discipline, is cumulative. The weight you lift this week is directly correlated to the weight you lifted the previous week and so on down the line when it comes to developing strength, power, and muscle. No shortcuts and no exceptions exist.

- *Concentration*: Concentration is an often overlooked aspect of strength training. It is, however, of paramount importance. You must aspire to bring full concentration to every exercise, set, and repetition during your strength workout. Full concentration, of course, is easier said than done, given the fact that the mind can wander off in a million different directions. Unlike participating in a softball game or practice, where concentration comes about naturally due to outside stimuli, training with weights is a personal undertaking that requires constant and mindful attention. So, keep your concentration focused on the task at hand in the weight room and watch as your workouts become ever more productive.

- *Breathing*: Typically, you will find it easier to inhale during the lowering phase of an exercise and breath out during the lifting or work phase of the movement. Many athletes and trainers have found that when working out with weights their breathing tends to regulate naturally without much conscious thought. Obviously, you should never hold your breath when lifting weights.

- *Rest between sets*: How much you rest between strength training sets mostly relates to how heavy you are lifting. During heavy training sessions, you should rest up to three minutes before attempting a subsequent set. If you're working with light or medium weights, anywhere from one to two minutes is the norm. Mixing up your rest intervals over the course of a workout is a great way to keep your muscles guessing and often leads to strength gains.

- *Lifting speed*: When it comes to the speed of individual repetitions, many contrasting views exist. Some experts feel that lifting in rapid fashion is more conducive to the needs of a softball player. Others believe that slower lifting allows a larger number of muscle fibers in to play, thus developing more strength. Somewhere in the middle of these two camps is best for most. Unless you're executing explosive-type lifts, such as hang cleans or high pulls that require high levels of repetition speed or specialized techniques like forced or negative repetitions where slow repetitions are employed, it is recommended that you lift in a powerful, yet controlled, manner without sacrificing proper exercise form.

- *Muscle balance*: While some areas of the body are more essential to softball performance than others, it is nevertheless of paramount importance that you achieve balanced muscular development. When antagonist muscle groups, such as hamstrings and quadriceps, are out of balance strength wise, coordination and performance can suffer. You also become more vulnerable to injury.

- *Record keeping*: It is extremely important that you maintain regular and accurate records concerning your strength training. At the very least, you should keep a training log that includes the date of workouts, exercises, exercise order, weights used, total sets, repetitions per set, rest between sets, and workout duration.

- *Variety*: Never has the saying, "variety is the spice of life," been more appropriate as when it relates to strength training. Mixing up your workout routine is essential to continued progress. A number of reasons can be listed to support this factor.

  First, changing your routine periodically keeps your muscles off balance, forcing them to adjust to the new demands placed upon them, thus producing gains in strength and power. The body adapts fairly quickly, especially if you've been training consistently for a while, and must be constantly challenged with new stimuli to improve.

  Second, incorporating different exercises, set sequences, repetition schemes, and training intensities enables your workouts to be more interesting and creative. The tediousness of performing the same workout week after week and month after month can take its toll on the attitude of even the most dedicated athlete.

  Finally, being flexible with your strength training will also help you avoid overuse injuries. Working muscles and joints from the same angle with the same movements for an extended number of workouts will eventually lead to injury.

- *Limitations*: No matter how great your potential, at some point, you will hit your strength limit. It may seem odd to bring up the topic of limitations in a book dedicated to improvement, but realizing your strengths and weaknesses (and even your limits) is an important factor in getting the most out of your strength program. Having unrealistic expectations can be almost as dangerous to your progress as setting lackluster goals. You must understand that genetics, like it or not, play a major role in muscle and strength development.

Training the Core

The power for all explosive athletic movements either emanates from or is transferred through the core of the body (midsection, hips, and lower back). Because of this, it is the most important part of the physique when it comes to softball performance. A strong core also contributes to the prevention of injury. Not surprisingly, core training will be a focal point of a softball player's strength program.

Core Training Secrets and Suggestions

- *Core strength comes first*: A solid base of core conditioning should be attained prior to engaging in intense full-body strength training. One way to achieve this is to focus intently on core-specific movements for the first four weeks or so of your off-season strength program. It is suggested that all softball players have a minimum of six lower back and 10 to 12 abdominal training sessions under their belts before stepping into a squat rack or lifting a loaded barbell overhead.

- *Strengthen the core gradually*: Core strengthening should always be undertaken in a gradual manner. Progressing too fast, especially with training for the sensitive lower back region, will put you at risk of injury. Unlike many other workout-related injuries, lower back ailments can become chronic and keep you out of action for extended periods of time. So, take care to move ahead deliberately with your core training by first focusing on the simpler, less taxing movements such as crunches, floor back raises, and light weight good mornings, before moving on to more complicated and demanding exercises like weighted prone hyper-extensions and hanging leg raises.

- *The midsection can be trained more frequently than the lower back and hips*: The lower back and hips can take considerable time to recover from intense training. A minimum of 72 hours and up to 96 hours between hip/lower back workouts may be necessary for some. On the other hand, abdominal muscles recover quite rapidly and can be exercised up to 5 days per week at reasonable levels of intensity. (Some elite, highly conditioned athletes actually train their mid sections on a daily basis.) In light of these recovery variables, it is recommended that softball players train the low back and hips no more than twice per week, while exercising the midsection at least four days per week. Adhering to this core training schedule will ensure strength balance, along with preventing overtraining-related injury.

- *Combine direct lower back work with leg training*: Multi-joint leg exercises such as squats and straight-legged dead lifts work the entire lower back region significantly. In fact, regardless of how strong your hips, quadriceps, and hamstrings are, a weak lower back will ensure that you'll never reach your full potential in these important lifts. Considering how the lower back, hips, and legs work in tandem both in the weight room and on the softball field, it is strongly suggested that you train these areas of the body together in the same workout. Perform the more energy intensive movement (squats, lunges, step-ups, etc.) first in the session, followed by direct lower back exercises like good mornings, reverse back raises, prone hyperextensions, etc.

- *Feel the burn*: While most strength and conditioning experts don't subscribe to the "no pain, no gain" theory of physical conditioning these days, an exception should be made with abdominal training. When you exercise your midsection, the goal is to feel the muscles work—burn, if you will. This unpleasant sensation signals that the muscles of the midsection are contracting sufficiently and is a necessary evil for productive abdominal workouts. Keep in mind also that athletes with disparate body types may respond differently to the same abdominal movements. Your responsibility is to find out which midsection exercises work best for you and act accordingly. This anti-one-size-fit-all approach to abdominal training will ensure that your midsection becomes strong, toned, and, above all, functional.

8

Core, Body Weight/Medicine Ball, and Upper Body Exercises

Core Exercises

Bench Crunch

Muscles worked: Upper abdominal region

Exercise type: Single-joint

Movement execution: Lying on your back with your hands clasped behind your head, place your feet and lower legs over a flat exercise bench. Proceed to sit up, raising your head toward your knees. Pause momentarily at the top of the movement and lower your body under control back to the floor.

Training tips and variations: This exercise can be performed without a bench by placing your feet flat on the floor with your legs bent at the knees. When executing crunches in this manner, make sure and concentrate on pushing your lower back into the floor or mat on the up phase of the movement. Numerous exercise machines also simulate the crunching motion; however, the floor version is more effective for most. For added resistance, you can hold a barbell plate or medicine ball behind your head.

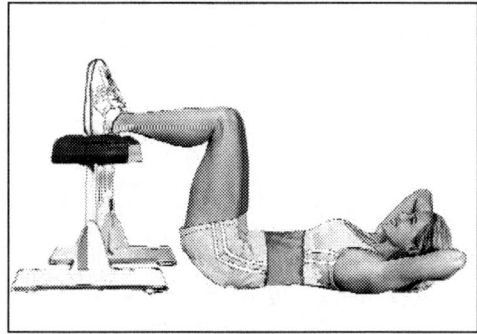 

Straight Legged Toe Touches

Muscles worked: Lower abdominal region

Exercise type: Single-joint

Movement execution: Lying on your back with your arms extended upward, hold your legs straight in the air as high as possible. From there, reach up and touch your toes, simultaneously contracting your lower abdominal muscles. This exercise should be performed in a quick, explosive manner.

Training tips and variations: Although your concentration during this movement should be on exercising your lower abdominal area, you can, by bending your knees slightly and positioning your legs forward, train your upper midsection more directly.

Medicine Ball Leg Lift

Muscles worked: Lower abdominal region

Exercise type: Single-joint

Movement execution: Lie on your back with your hands clasped behind your head and raise your legs to the vertical position. Place an appropriately weighted medicine ball between your legs just above your knees. Begin by lowering your legs in a controlled manner to just short of the floor, pause briefly, and proceed to lift your legs, medicine ball in tow, back up to the vertical position.

Training tips and variations: Novice trainers can substitute a volleyball or basketball for a medicine ball during this exercise. Some feel that squeezing the legs together during execution of medicine ball leg lifts increases the tension on the abdominal muscles.

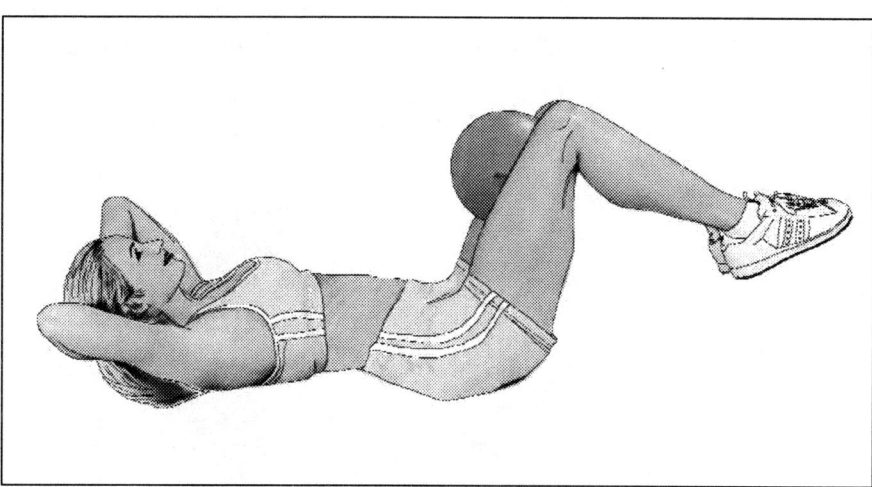

Medicine Ball Twist

Muscles worked: Entire abdominal region and obliques

Exercise type: Single-joint

Movement execution: Lie on your back with your knees slightly bent and your feet raised off the floor approximately six inches. Grab an appropriately weighted medicine ball and hold it at your midsection a few inches above your body. Then, while keeping your knees bent and your legs off the floor, raise your torso up until you're balancing on your tailbone. Proceed to swing from your midsection while maintaining a stationary torso and touch the ball to the floor. Continue back and forth for the required number of repetitions.

Training tips and variations: To lessen the intensity of this exercise, plant your feet firmly on the ground as opposed to having them in the air. Beginners may want to use a volleyball or basketball in lieu of a medicine ball for this exercise until their strength level improves.

Bicycle Sit-Up

Muscles worked: Entire abdominal region and obliques

Exercise type: Single-joint

Movement execution: Lying on your back with your hands lightly touching the back of your head and your legs two to three feet off the ground, proceed to sit-up, while simultaneously bringing your right elbow to your left knee. Return to the starting position and repeat by bringing your left elbow to your right knee. Continue to alternate in this manner for the required number of repetitions.

Training tips and variations: Some advanced athletes may want to incorporate a medicine ball in this exercise by moving it from knee to knee during execution.

Hip-Up

Muscles worked: Lower abdominal region

Exercise type: Single-joint

Movement execution: Begin by lying on your back on a flat exercise bench and bring your knees to your chest. Take hold of the bench with both hands positioned over your head. Proceed to drive your hips and legs up in the air as high as you can. Pause briefly at the top and then return to the starting position.

Training tips and variations: If a bench is not available, this exercise can be performed on the floor while grabbing a stationary object with both hands behind your head. Some advanced trainers may want to add resistance to hip-ups by wearing a pair of ankle weights during execution.

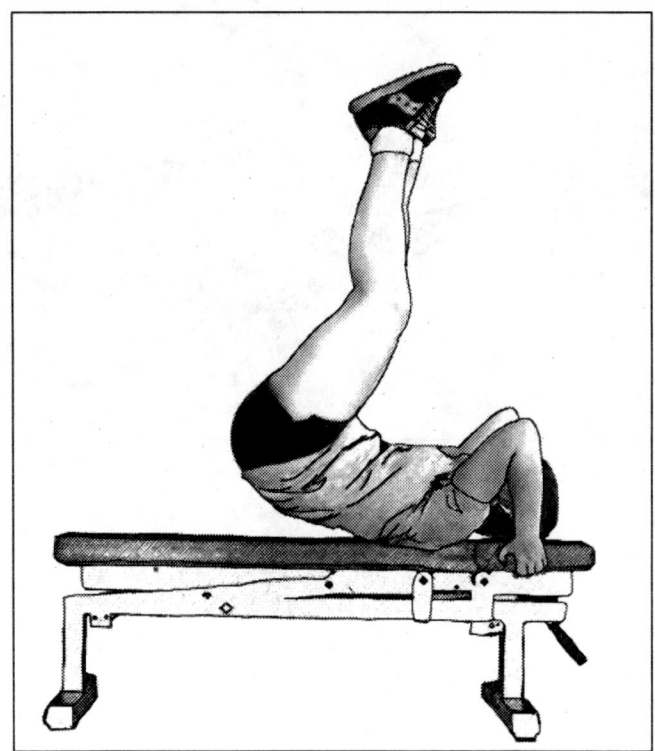

Hanging Leg Raise

Muscles worked: Lower abdominal region

Exercise type: Single-joint

Movement execution: Start by hanging at arm's length from a chinning bar with an overhand, shoulder-width grip. Proceed to lift your legs straight out in front of you, while keeping your hips and torso as stationary as possible. Hold for a count at the contracted position and return by lowering your legs back to the starting position.

Training tips and variations: Some trainers use grip-enhancing straps when performing hanging leg raises. You can also execute this movement on a vertical bench, where you support yourself by the elbows, thus taking the grip element completely out of the equation. To lessen the intensity of the exercise, bend your knees during the up phase of the movement.

Floor Back Raise

Muscles worked: Entire lower back region

Exercise type: Single-joint

Movement execution: Lying face down on the floor, slowly raise your legs and trunk in unison as high as possible. Hold for a two count at the contracted position and then slowly lower back to the relaxed position.

Training tips and variations: This exercise can be executed by raising one leg and one arm at a time (left leg, right arm; right leg, left arm) for variety.

Prone Hyperextension

Muscles worked: Entire lower back region and hamstrings

Exercise type: Multi-joint

Movement execution: Position yourself so that you are facedown across a hyperextension bench, with your feet underneath the footpads. With your arms folded across your chest or clasped behind your neck, bend straight down from the waist over the pad. Then, come back up under control until your torso is approximately parallel to the ground.

Training tips and variations: Before training on a hyperextension bench, it is suggested that you first develop a base of lower back strength by performing floor back raises. Resistance can be added to this exercise by holding a barbell plate, dumbbell, or medicine ball across your chest or behind your neck.

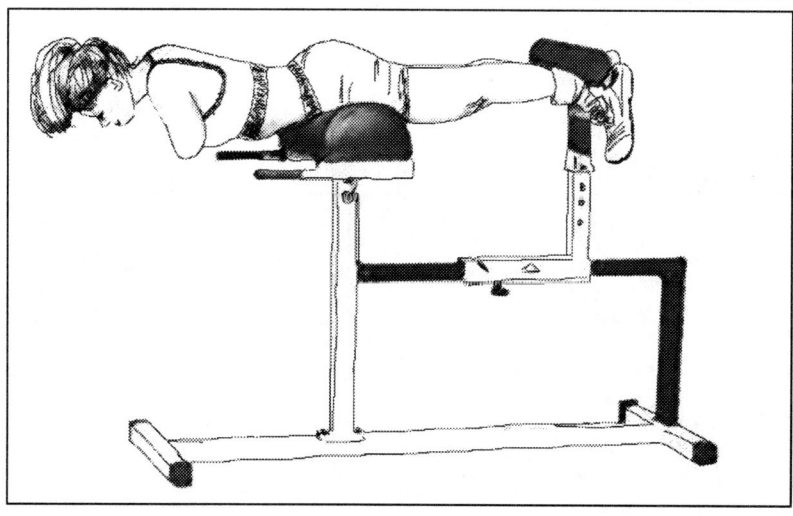

Good Morning

Muscles worked: Entire lower back region and hamstrings

Exercise type: Multi-joint

Movement execution: Standing with you feet close together, hold an appropriately weighted barbell behind your neck. Keeping your legs and back straight, bend at the waist until your upper body is approximately parallel to the floor. Pause briefly, then rise up under control to the standing position.

Training tips and variations: This exercise should be performed with reasonably light weights. Some beginners may feel more comfortable executing good mornings with a broomstick instead of a barbell until their strength level increases.

Reverse Back Raises

Muscles worked: Entire lower back region

Exercise type: Single-joint

Movement execution: Lean over a hyperextension bench so that the pad supports your midsection and pelvis. (You'll be facing the opposite direction as you would during prone hyperextensions.) Grasp the rollers with your hands and let your legs hang down naturally. Proceed to lift your legs and pelvis in a controlled motion until your legs are slightly higher than your back. Hold for a count and then return to the starting position.

Training tips and variations: Some advanced athletes add resistance to reverse back raises by wearing ankle weights or holding a light dumbbell between their ankles.

Machine Back Extension

Muscles worked: Entire lower back region

Exercise type: Single-joint

Movement execution: Sit comfortably in a lower back machine so that your pelvis is solidly positioned against the back cushion. Proceed to bend backward under control as far as the machine (and your body) allows. Hold for a two count and then return to the starting position.

Training tips and variations: Machine back extensions should always be performed in a deliberate and careful manner. Moving backward too quickly puts you at risk for possible injury. Many variations of this machine exist. Execution instructions are the same for all.

Body Weight and Medicine Ball Exercises

Body Weight Squat

Muscles worked: Hips, quadriceps, buttocks, hamstrings, and lower back

Exercise type: Multi-joint

Movement execution: Standing with your feet approximately shoulder width apart and pointed slightly outward, proceed to bend at the knees and lower yourself down until your upper legs are just below parallel to the floor. Keeping your head up and back straight, drive yourself back up to the standing position.

Training tips and variations: When performing squats, it is important that your knees remain behind your toes throughout the movement. To increase difficulty, you can execute this exercise while wearing a weighted vest or holding a medicine ball at arm's length in front of you.

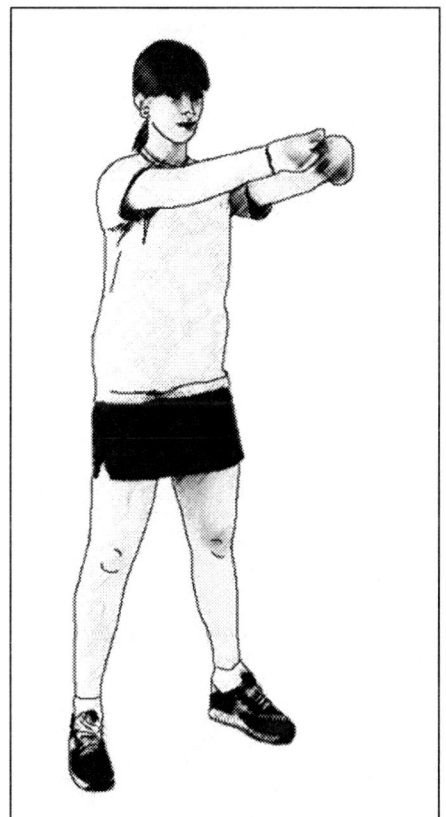
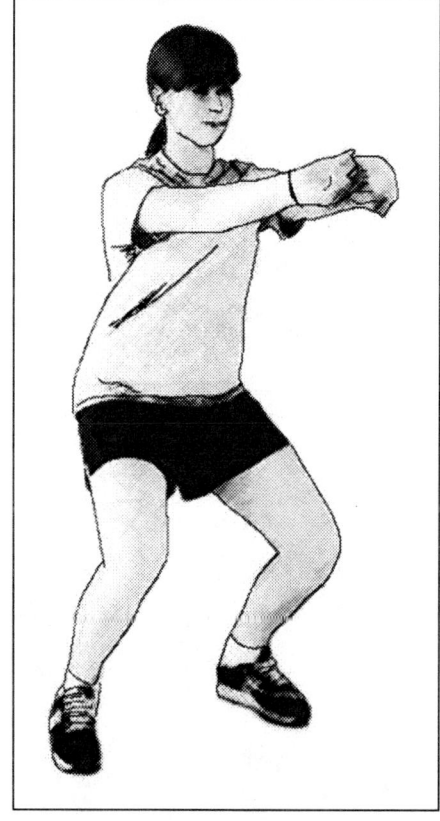

Inverted Chin-Up

Muscles worked: Latisimus dorsi, biceps, and forearms

Exercise type: Multi-joint

Movement execution: Place your heels on a raised surface such as an exercise bench or step and hang at arm's length with an overhand grip from a bar secured on a racked bench. Proceed to pull yourself up until the bar is directly under your chin. Lower under control to the starting position and repeat.

Training tips and variations: This exercise can be performed with an underhand grip for variety. To increase the difficulty of inverted chin-ups, place your heals on a fitness ball instead of a bench or step. A smith machine can be used in lieu of a conventional bar and bench.

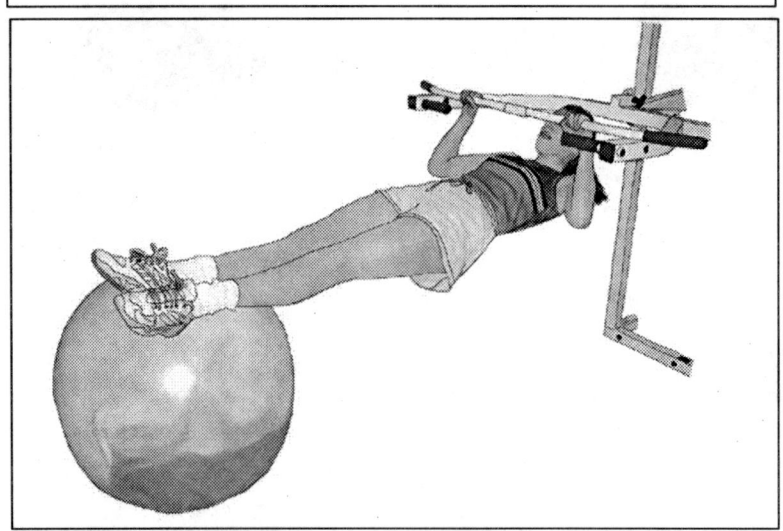

Push-Up

Muscles worked: Middle chest, anterior deltoids, and triceps

Exercise type: Multi-joint

Movement execution: Assume a conventional push-up position, which entails facing the floor with your hands planted firmly on the ground at shoulder width/chest level and your legs fully extended with your feet close together. Begin by rising up to the arms extended position (starting position) and proceed to lower yourself down until your chest is within a few inches of the floor. From the low position, powerfully push up by extending your arms.

Training tips and variations: Push-ups can be made more difficult by raising your feet on a step or bench; wearing resistance equipment, such as a weighted vest; or incorporating specially designed push-up bars, which allow for increased range of motion. To lessen the intensity of the exercise, balance your lower body on your knees instead of your toes.

Wall Slide

Muscles worked: Quadriceps, hips, buttocks, and hamstrings

Exercise type: Multi-joint

Movement execution: Position your straight back against a wall with your knees bent at approximately 120 degrees and your feet planted firmly on the floor positioned slightly wider than shoulder width. With your back maintaining contact with the wall, slide down under control until your upper legs are parallel to the floor (approximately 90-degree angle). Pause for a five count at the bottom and then proceed to push yourself back to the starting position.

Training tips and variations: To increase the intensity of wall slides, hold a appropriately weighted medicine ball at arms length directly out in front of you during execution.

Medicine Ball Push Press

Muscles worked: Upper chest, anterior deltoids, triceps, quadriceps, hips, and lower back

Exercise type: Multi-joint

Movement execution: In a standing position, grab an appropriately weighted medicine ball and rest it on your upper chest just below your neck. Begin by bending at the knees and then simultaneously straighten your legs and push the ball straight up overhead to the arms-extended position. Lower under control to the starting position.

Training tips and variations: To incorporate more of your lower body when executing push presses, bend all the way to the full squat position (upper legs approximately parallel to the ground) before rising up and pushing the resistance overhead.

Bench Dip

Muscles worked: Triceps, entire shoulder girdle, and lower chest

Exercise type: Multi-joint

Movement execution: Sit in the middle of an exercise bench with your hands at your sides and your legs extended in front of you. While balancing on your heels, proceed to lift yourself off the bench and then, by bending at the elbows, lower your body down as far as possible. Once in the low position, pause briefly and then powerfully push yourself up until your arms are fully extended.

Training Tips and variations: To add intensity to this exercise, place a light medicine ball or barbell plate on your lap during execution.

Medicine Ball Chest Press

Muscles worked: Middle chest, anterior deltoids, and triceps

Exercise type: Multi-joint

Movement execution: Lie on your back either on the floor or on a flat exercise bench. Take hold of an appropriately weighted medicine ball and rest it at mid-chest level. With a training partner standing directly above you, proceed to powerfully press and toss the ball straight up to your partner.

Training tips and variations: If a training partner is not available, you can catch the ball yourself after the press and toss.

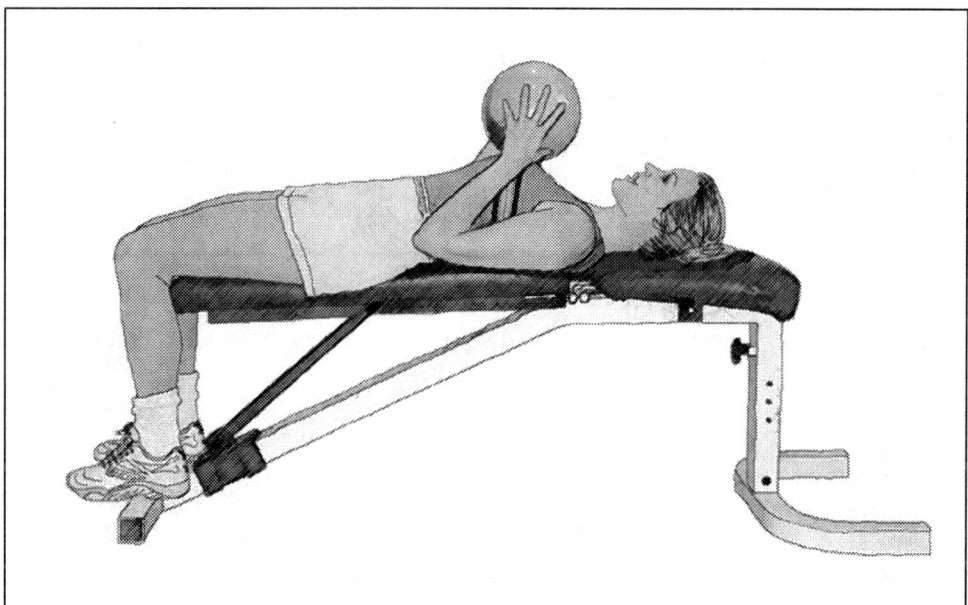

Upper Body Exercises

Bench Press

Muscles worked: Middle chest, anterior deltoids, and triceps

Exercise type: Multi-joint

Movement execution: Lying on your back on a flat exercise bench with your hands slightly wider than shoulder width, lift a loaded barbell off a rack and hold it with your arms extended above you. With your feet planted firmly on the ground and your buttocks tight against the bench, lower the weight under control to your mid-chest. Pause briefly and proceed to press the bar back up to the locked-out position.

Training tips and variations: It is important that you keep your back as flat as possible to the bench during the execution of this movement (no arching). Arching your back, while enabling you to lift more weight, takes away the intent of the exercise and could cause lower back injury. The bench press can be performed with dumbbells or on a variety of machines.

Incline Press

Muscles worked: Upper chest, anterior deltoids, and triceps

Exercise type: Multi-joint

Movement execution: Lying on an incline bench (approximately 45-degree incline), take a loaded barbell off the rack. Your grip should be slightly closer than that of the bench press (roughly shoulder width). Lower the weight to your upper chest just below your neck. Pause briefly and proceed to press the resistance back up to the arms locked position.

Training tips and variations: It is important when performing incline presses to avoid the tendency to press the weight out instead of up. Let the position of the bench take care of the direction of the weight and make sure to lift the resistance straight up on each and every repetition. As with the bench press, this exercise can be performed with dumbbells and on a variety of machines.

 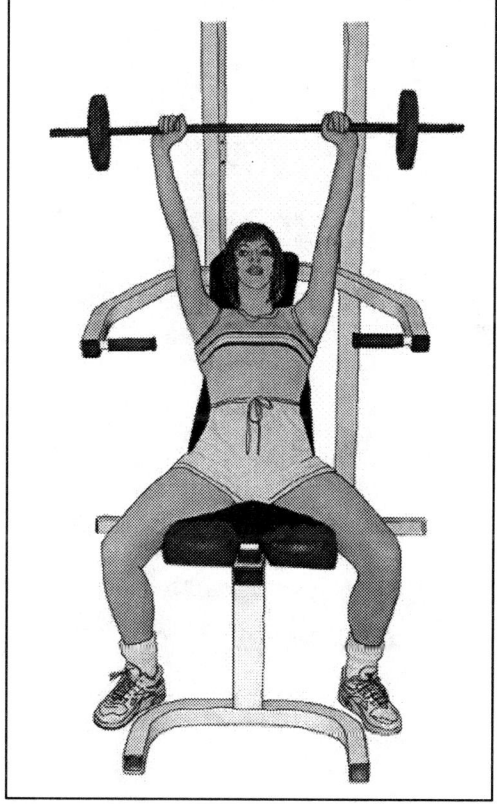

Dip

Muscles worked: Lower chest, anterior deltoids, and triceps

Exercise type: Multi-joint

Movement execution: Start by balancing at arm's length above a dipping bar or parallel bars. Lower yourself under control until your shoulders are slightly above the bars. Then push upward forcefully to the arm's extended position.

Training tips and variations: To make dips more difficult, you can add resistance by wearing a weighted vest or placing a dumbbell between your crossed ankles during execution. To lessen intensity, dips can be performed on a Gravitron machine, where a percentage of your body weight can be used.

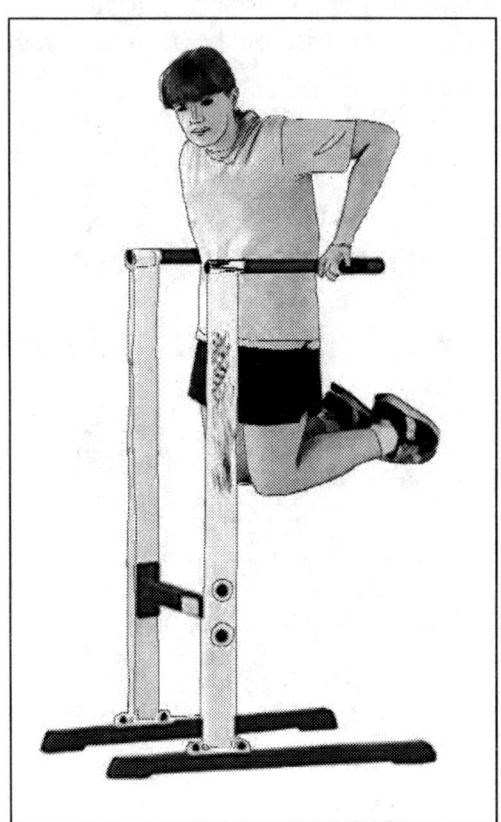
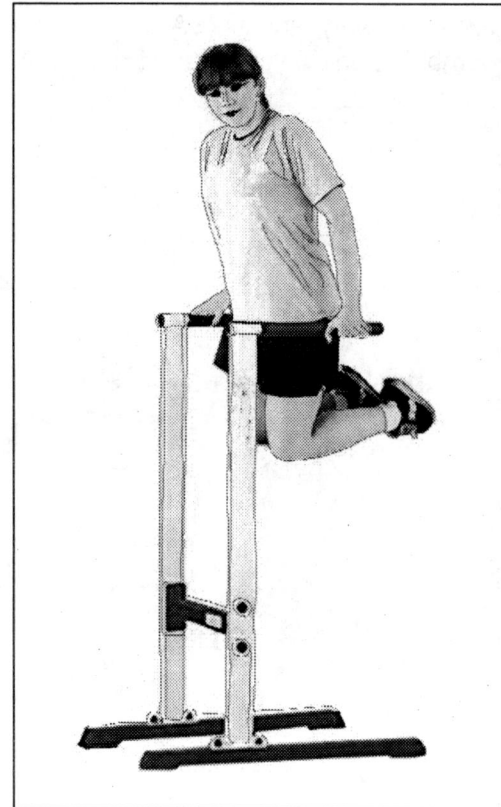

Dumbbell Shoulder Press

Muscles worked: Anterior deltoids, medial deltoids, and triceps

Exercise type: Multi-joint

Movement execution: Seated on a flat exercise bench, grab hold of a dumbbell in each hand and position the weights at shoulder height, with elbows out at your sides and palms facing forward. Lift the dumbbells straight up to the arm's extended position, hold for a count, and lower the resistance back to the starting position.

Training tips and variations: This exercise can be performed with a barbell or on a variety of machines. If you have shoulder or neck problems, however, barbell shoulder presses should be avoided.

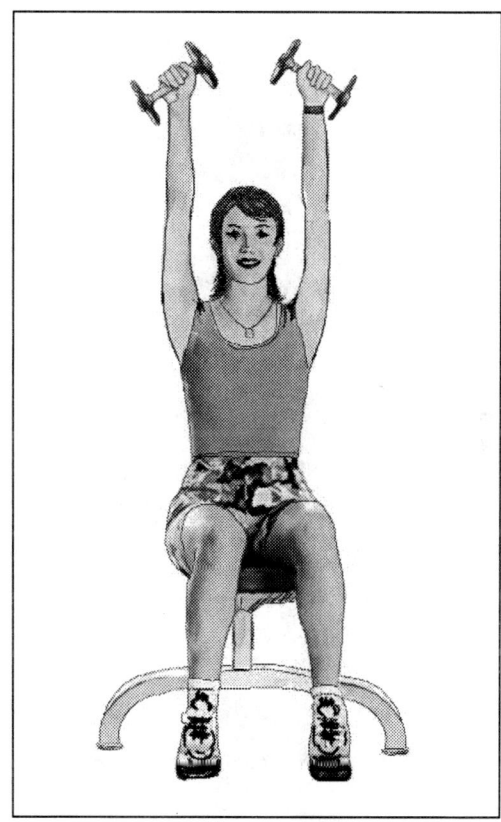

Upright Row

Muscles worked: Trapezius, medial deltoids, posterior deltoids, biceps, and forearms

Exercise type: Multi-joint

Movement execution: In a standing position, grasp a loaded barbell with an overhand grip. Your hands should be positioned on the bar between five to eight inches apart. Starting with your arms extended, lift the resistance straight up, keeping the bar as close to your body as possible, to a point just below your chin. Pause briefly and then lower the bar under control back to the arm's extended position.

Training tips and variations: To involve more of the deltoids when performing upright rows, widen your grip to 10 to 12 inches. To exercise the trapezius more fully, narrow your grip to an inch or two. This movement can be executed with a floor pulley for variety.

Lateral Raise

Muscles worked: Medial deltoids

Exercise type: Single-joint

Movement execution: Standing with your knees slightly flexed, take hold of two moderately weighted dumbbells and position them at your sides. Proceed to raise the weights with slightly bent elbows in unison away from your sides, until your arms are just above parallel to the ground. Lower the dumbbells slowly back to the starting position, consciously resting the weight on the way down.

Training tips and variations: Lateral raises can be executed seated as well as standing. A number of machines can be used for this exercise.

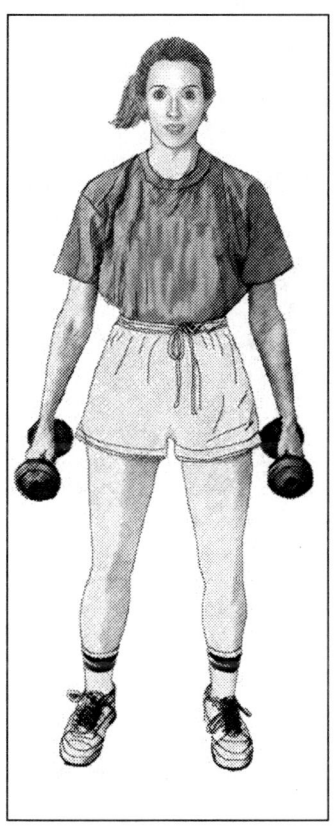

Bent Lateral Raise

Muscles worked: Posterior deltoids

Exercise type: Single-joint

Movement execution: Seated near the end of a flat exercise bench, lean over at the waist and grab two fairly light dumbbells from the floor. Keeping your body balanced and your head down, lift the weights out to either side, turning your wrists so that your thumbs are pointed downward. Your arms will be slightly bent throughout, and the dumbbells should be lifted to just above head height before descending to the starting position.

Training tips and variations: For best results, bent lateral raises should be performed with light weights. This exercise can be executed standing while bending at the waist, lying prone over an incline bench, or on a variety of machines.

Chin-Up

Muscles worked: Upper latisimus dorsi, posterior deltoids, biceps, and forearms

Exercise type: Multi-joint

Movement execution: Grab hold of a chinning bar with an overhand grip and hang down at arm's length. Your hands should be spaced several inches wider than shoulder width. Pull yourself up so that the bar touches your upper chest. Proceed to lower yourself down under control to the arm's extended position.

Training tips and variations: When performing conventional chin-ups, arching your back slightly during the concentric (pulling up) portion of the movement is suggested. This action will ensure that you stress the upper back muscles fully. This exercise has many variations, including bringing the bar to the back of your neck, using an underhand grip, or incorporating a double-handled bar. Beginners may want execute this exercise on a Gravitron machine, where a percentage of your body weight can be used.

Dumbbell Row

Muscles worked: Middle and lower latisimus dorsi, posterior deltoids, biceps, and forearms

Exercise type: Multi-joint

Movement execution: Place one hand and one knee on a flat exercise bench. Grab a sufficiently heavy dumbbell from the floor and, keeping your back flat and your grounded foot firmly based, lift the weight up to your side. Squeeze your back muscles at the top of the movement and then proceed to lower the resistance smoothly back to the floor.

Training tips and variations: Because the lower back is supported during dumbbell rows, it is possible to incorporate very heavy weights in this exercise without fear of injury. For variety, this movement can be executed on a variety of machines.

Pull-Down

Muscles worked: Upper latisimus dorsi, posterior deltoids, biceps, and forearms

Exercise type: Multi-joint

Movement execution: Incorporating a lat machine, grab the bar with a fairly wide, overhand grip. Then, arching your back slightly, pull the bar down until it touches the top of your chest. Pause briefly and proceed to extend your arms back to the starting position.

Training tips and variations: Similar to chin-ups, it is possible to use a variety of hand placements when performing pull-downs. Unlike chin-ups, you can exercise with less than your own body weight.

Triceps Press Down

Muscles worked: Triceps

Exercise type: Single-joint

Movement execution: Grasp a short bar from an overhead pulley with an overhand grip and your hands six to eight inches apart. With your elbows close to your torso and your knees slightly flexed, push the bar down, locking your elbows at the bottom. Release and then bring the resistance back to the starting point (approximately mid-chest height) before repeating.

Training tips and variations: For variety, you can use a v-shaped bar, a specially designed rope, or a lat machine for triceps press-downs. Also, you can experiment with different hand spacings or incorporate an underhand grip, which promotes additional stretch.

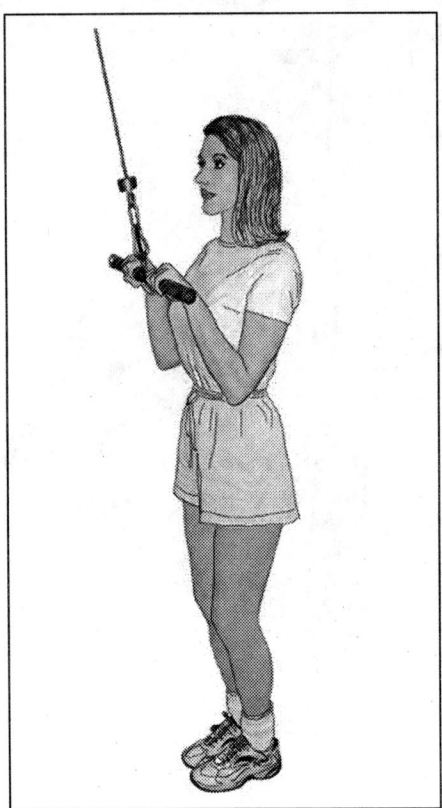
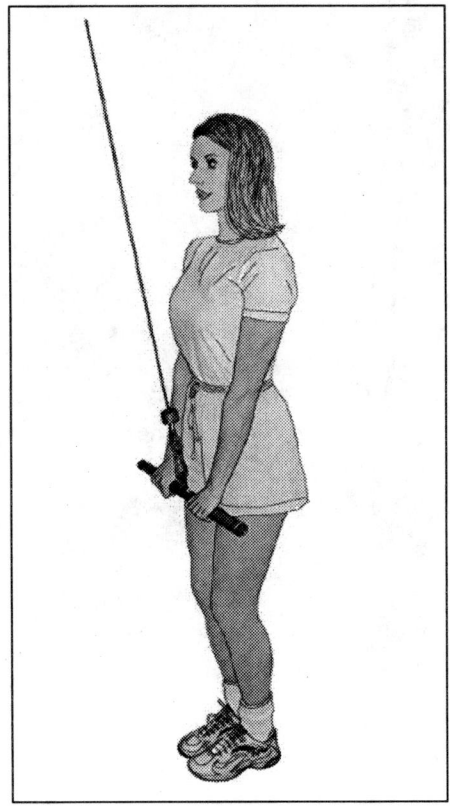

Lying Triceps Extension

Muscles worked: Triceps

Exercise type: Single-joint

Movement execution: Lying on a flat exercise bench with your head just off the edge, take hold of an appropriately weighted barbell with a slightly closer than shoulder-width grip and place it above your forehead. Keeping your elbows stationary, push the resistance up by extending your arms to the lock out position. Then, lower the bar carefully back to the starting position.

Training tips and variations: Many trainers feel that using an E-Z curl bar (a specially shaped bar that allows for increased grip stability) when performing lying triceps extensions gives more control and a slightly increased range of motion. If you don't have access to a bench, this exercise can be executed while lying flat on the floor.

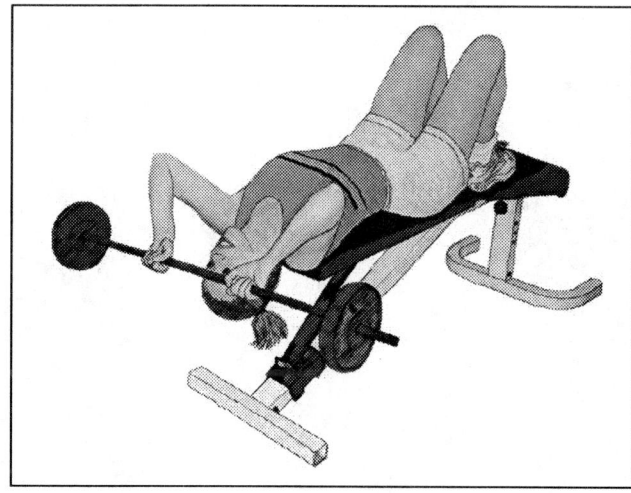

Barbell Curl

Muscles worked: Biceps

Exercise type: Single-joint

Movement execution: Standing with your knees slightly flexed, grasp a loaded barbell off a waist-high rack with an underhand, shoulder-width grip. Let the bar hang down with your arms straight and then curl the weight up smoothly to the upper chest, keeping your back straight and your elbows close to your torso. Pause at the top and proceed to lower the resistance back down to the starting position.

Training tips and variations: In order to squeeze out a few extra repetitions, a small amount of body swing is acceptable during this movement. A floor pulley or dumbbells can be used in lieu of a barbell for variety.

Incline Dumbbell Curl

Muscles worked: Upper biceps

Exercise type: Single-joint

Movement execution: Seated on an incline bench, hold a dumbbell in each hand with your arms fully extended and your palms facing each other. With your elbows in, curl both dumbbells in unison, while slowly twisting your palms upward, to your front deltoids. Then, lower the weights slowly back down to the starting position.

Training tips and variations: It is important that you pause at the bottom of the movement to prevent yourself from using momentum for the next repetition. The dumbbells can be lifted one at a time for variety.

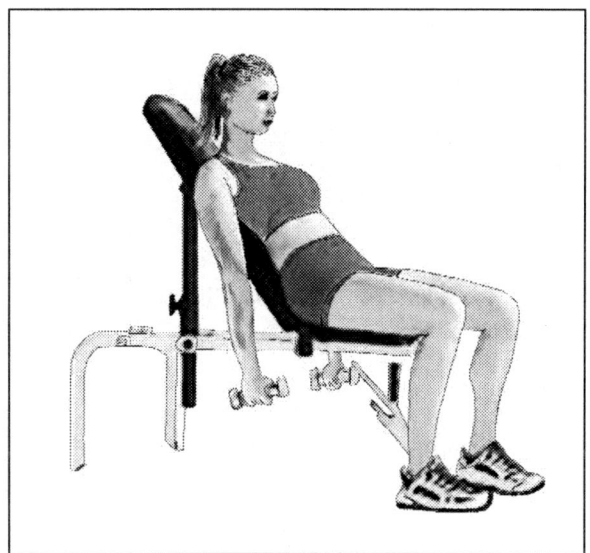

9

Lower Body, Combination, and Softball Specific Exercises

Lower Body Exercises

Squat

Muscles worked: Hips, quadriceps, buttocks, hamstrings, and lower back

Exercise type: Multi-joint

Movement execution: Standing with your feet approximately shoulder-width apart and pointed slightly outward, rest a loaded barbell across your shoulders behind your neck. With your hands balancing the bar, bend your knees and lower yourself until your upper legs are just below parallel to the floor. Keeping your head up and your back straight, drive yourself back up to the standing position.

Training tips and variations: When performing squats, it is important that you keep your knees behind your toes throughout the movement. Not doing so leaves you vulnerable to knee stress. Also, if you've never squatted before, it is advisable to use light weight until you feel comfortable with the movement. Dumbbells resting on the front of your shoulders can be used in lieu of a barbell for variety.

Leg Press

Muscles worked: Quadriceps, hips, buttocks, and hamstrings

Exercise type: Multi-joint

Movement execution: Seated in a leg press machine, place your feet near the top of the foot piece, with your toes pointed slightly outward and your legs approximately shoulder-width apart. Unlock the weight and bend at the knees, lowering the resistance as far as possible. Press the weight back up through your heels to just short of the legs-extended position.

Training tips and variations: It is suggested that you do not lock your knees at the top of the leg press. This strategy allows you to maintain tension on your thighs throughout the movement. A variety of leg press machines are available for your use. The same training principles apply to all.

Lunge

Muscles worked: Quadriceps, buttocks, hips, hamstrings, and calves

Exercise type: Multi-joint

Movement execution: Standing upright and holding a barbell across your shoulders behind your neck, step forward, bend at the knees, and bring your rear knee close to the floor. Then, proceed by driving yourself powerfully back up to the standing position.

Training tips and variations: Lunges can be performed by alternating legs every repetition or by doing separate sets for each leg. Separate-leg sets are suggested, as they work the lower body muscles more intensely. Dumbbells held at your sides can also be used for this movement.

Straight-Legged Dead Lift

Muscles worked: Hamstrings and lower back

Exercise type: Multi-joint

Movement execution: While standing, take hold of a barbell with an overhand, shoulder-width grip. Keeping your legs straight, bend at the waist with your back flat and your arms extended. Pause momentarily when your torso is parallel to the floor (you will feel the pull in your hamstrings) and then straighten slowly back to the standing position.

Training tips and variations: It is best to perform straight-legged dead lifts in a deliberate manner, especially when incorporating heavy weights. Dumbbells or a floor pulley can be used in lieu of a barbell periodically for this exercise.

Front Squat

Muscles worked: Quadriceps, hips, buttocks, hamstrings, and lower back

Exercise type: Multi-joint

Movement execution: Place a loaded barbell at chest height on a rack. Step under the rack and position the bar across the front of your shoulders with your hands balancing the resistance. Your elbows should be rotated so that they are ahead of the bar. Step away from the rack and proceed to bend your knees, keeping your head up and back straight, and lower yourself until your upper legs are just below parallel to the floor. Pause briefly and explode upward to the starting position.

Training tips and variations: Some trainers prefer to cross their arms in front of their shoulders with their hands placed on top of the bar when executing front squats. This exercise can be performed with dumbbells or on a variety of machines. However, the barbell version of the front squat is far superior for strength development.

Step-Up

Muscles worked: Hips, quadriceps, buttocks, hamstrings, and calves

Exercise type: Multi-joint

Movement execution: With a barbell resting across your shoulders and your hands balancing the resistance, step up on to a box or step (the height of the box/step will vary depending on your stature, strength, and training objectives) as if you were climbing stairs. Pause at the top with your legs straight, and then step down carefully back to the floor.

Training tips and variations: Step-ups can be performed either by alternating legs every repetition or by doing one complete set with your left leg followed by one complete set with your right leg. For variety, step-ups can be executed with dumbbells or while wearing a weighted vest.

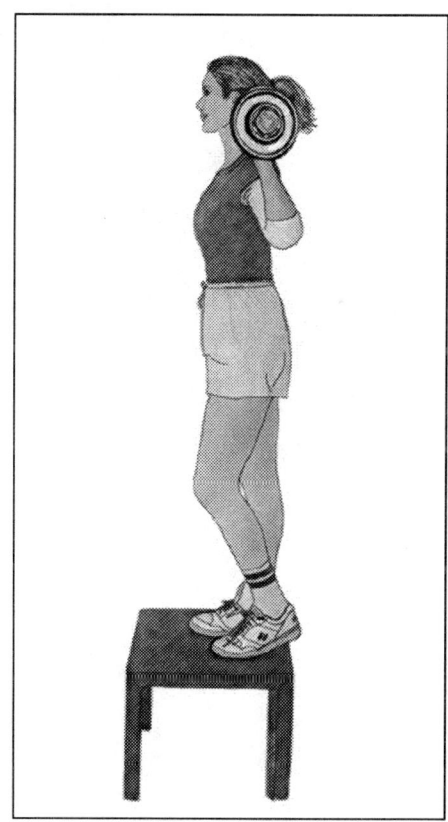

Leg Extension

Muscles worked: Quadriceps

Exercise type: Single-joint

Movement exection: Using a leg-extension machine, sit and anchor your feet under the cushions. Then, extend your lower legs up as high as possible and hold for a two count. Lower the weight under control to the starting position.

Training tips and variations: Leg extensions can be executed one leg at a time for variety.

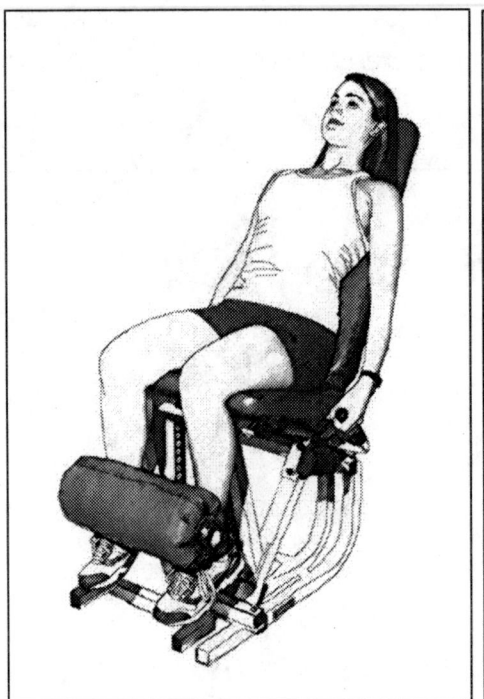 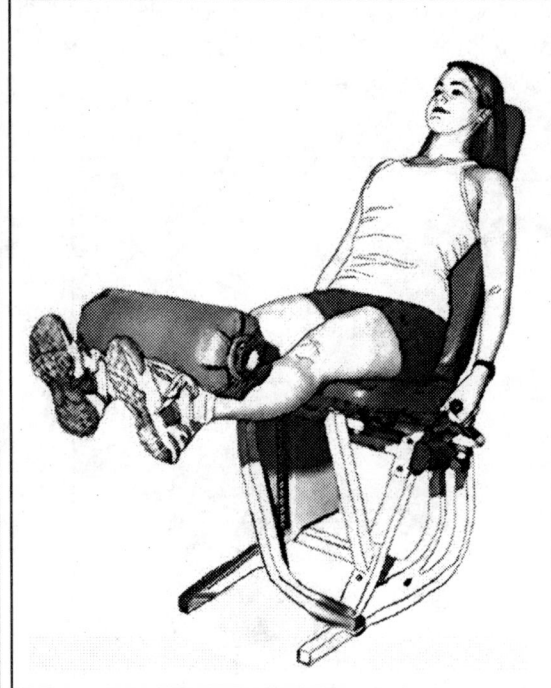

Leg Curl

Muscles worked: Hamstrings

Exercise type: Single-joint

Movement execution: Lying on your stomach on a leg-curl machine, place your heels under the pads. Using your hamstring muscles, pull your heels up as close as possible to your buttocks, while keeping your body flat on the machine. Pause for a count at the top and then lower the resistance back to the starting position.

Training tips and variations: As with leg extensions, leg curls can be performed one leg at a time for variety. In addition to the conventional leg curl machine, some gyms have equipment that allow you to isolate one leg at a time from a standing position.

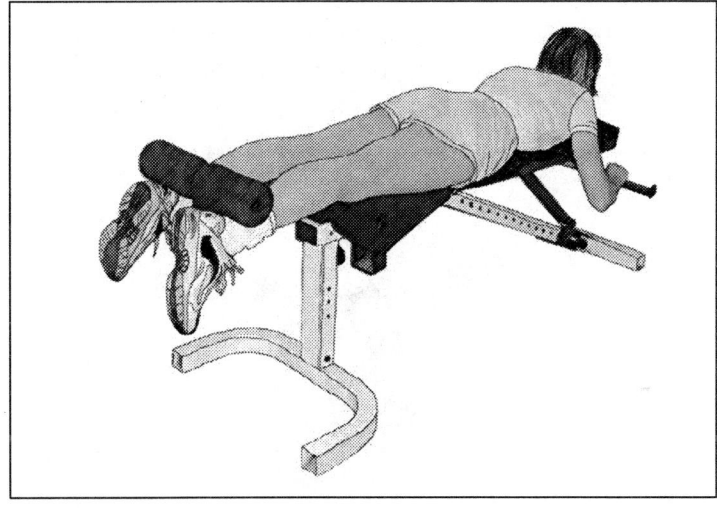

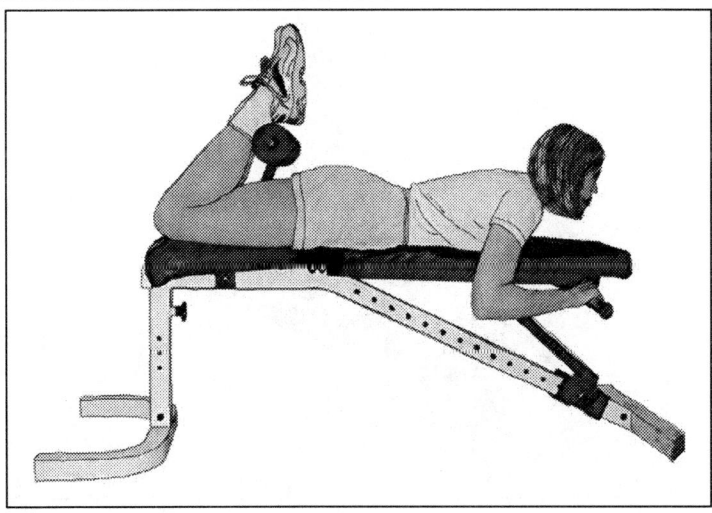

Standing Calve Raise

Muscles worked: Calves

Exercise type: Single-joint

Movement execution: Stand with your toes on a block or step with an appropriately weighted barbell resting across your shoulders. Your hands should hold the resistance in place. Proceed by lowering your heels as far as you can toward the ground, maintaining slightly flexed knees throughout. When you reach the fully stretched position, come up on your toes as high as possible. Hold at the top for a two count and repeat.

Training tips and variations: Since your calves are involved in almost every athletic activity (running, jumping, sliding, etc.), they develop quite a high tolerance for training. Therefore, calves can be exercised with extremely heavy weights. In lieu of the barbell version of this exercise, you can use a variety of standing calve raise machines. Dumbbells held in each hand can also be utilized for standing calve raises.

Combination Exercises

Push Press

Muscles worked: Upper chest, anterior deltoids, quadriceps, hips, lower back, and triceps

Exercise type: Multi-joint

Movement execution: In a standing position, grab a loaded barbell off a chest-high rack with a shoulder-width grip and rest it on your upper chest just below the neck. Start by bending your knees approximately halfway to parallel and simultaneously straighten your legs and push the weight straight up overhead to the arms-extended position. Lower the resistance slowly back to the starting position.

Training tips and variations: During the positive (lifting) phase of the push press, make sure to keep your body positioned under the weight. Not doing so could cause a loss of balance and possible injury. Dumbbells can be substituted for a barbell for variety.

High Pull

Muscles worked: Hips, quadriceps, lower back, calves, trapezius, medial deltoids, posterior deltoids, biceps, and forearms

Exercise type: Multi-joint

Movement execution: With an overhand, shoulder-width grip, grab a loaded barbell off a waist-high rack and position it on your lower thighs just above the knees. Your back should be flat, head straight, knees flexed, and feet hip-width apart. Proceed to explosively move the resistance upward by pulling with your arms and shrugging with your shoulders until the bar is just below your chin. The bar should remain close to your body throughout the upward movement. Your calves will raise in tandem with the bar. Lower the weight to the starting position and repeat.

Training tips and variations: You always want to keep your shoulders over the bar when executing high pulls. Dumbbells can be used in place of a barbell for this exercise, but the barbell version is most effective, thus should be incorporated for the majority of high pull workouts.

Hang Clean

Muscles worked: Hips, quadriceps, lower back, calves, anterior deltoids, medial deltoids, trapezius, forearms, and biceps

Exercise type: Multi-joint

Movement execution: Assume the same hand position (overhand, shoulder-width grip) and starting position (bar resting on your lower thighs) as you would when executing a high pull. Your back should be flat, head straight, knees flexed, and feet at hip-width apart. Proceed to extend your hips up and slightly forward, moving to the balls of your feet while shrugging your shoulders. Move under the bar, elevating your feet momentarily, and, while rotating your elbows, receive the bar on your anterior (front) deltoids. Make sure your knees and hips are sufficiently bent to absorb the resistance.

Training tips and variations: Most beginners should perfect their form by using a lighter object such as a broomstick for hang cleans.

Explosive Squat

Muscles worked: Hips, quadriceps, buttocks, lower back, hamstrings, and calves

Exercise type: Multi-joint

Movement execution: As with the conventional squat, stand with your feet approximately shoulder-width apart and toes pointed slightly outward and rest a loaded barbell across your shoulders. With your hands balancing the resistance, bend your knees and lower yourself so that your thighs are just below parallel to the floor. Keeping your head up and your back straight, explode powerfully up to the standing position, ending as high as possible on your toes. Lower to the flatfooted position, pause briefly, and repeat.

Training tips and variations: Although explosive squats are meant to be performed at a high rate of speed, it is still a priority that you maintain proper lifting form. Dumbbells can be substituted for a barbell in this movement for variety.

Softball Forearm Series

As anyone involved in the game of softball is well aware, forearm strength is crucial to successful hitting. The forearms, wrists, hands, and fingers must not only absorb the contact of the pitched softball, but be strong enough to transfer the swing power generated by the body's larger muscle groups through contact.

Following, the "Softball Forearm Series" is detailed. It includes four direct forearm exercises, all of which have proven to increase forearm strength dramatically. For best results, perform the movements as a group, one after the other in a circuit, resting no more than 20 seconds between each exercise. Beginners should start with one to two circuits. More advanced trainers are best served executing three to four complete circuits. The series should be performed at the end of your strength workout two to three days per week.

Hammer Curl

Muscles worked: Forearms and biceps

Exercise type: Single-joint

Movement execution: Seated at the end of a flat exercise bench, grasp a dumbbell in each hand. With your arms fully extended at your sides and your palms facing each other, curl the weights straight up to your front deltoids, keeping your wrists stationary throughout. Pause at the top and then lower the dumbbells under control back to the starting position.

Training tips and variations: Hammer curls can also be performed while standing.

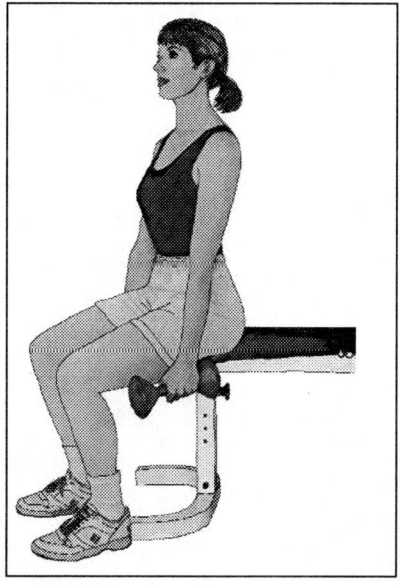 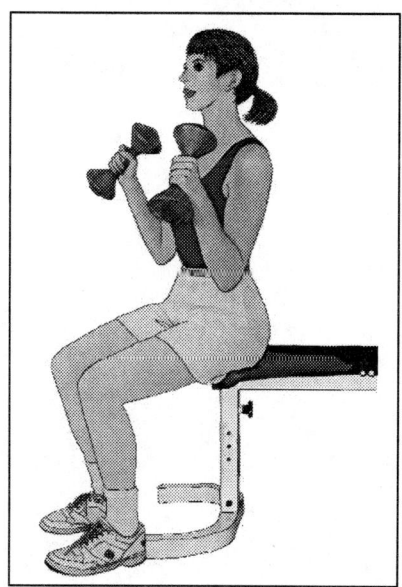

Wrist Curl

Muscles worked: Forearms

Exercise type: Single-joint

Movement execution: Take hold of a barbell or strength bar (a mini-barbell with the weight positioned in the middle of the short bar) with an underhand grip and your hands three to five inches apart. From there, take a kneeling position perpendicular to the middle of a flat exercise bench and place your forearms over the bench with your hands hanging just off the edge. Keeping your body stationary, proceed to lower your hands as far as you can and, at the bottom, reverse direction and bring the resistance back up as high as possible.

Training tips and variations: This exercise can be performed with dumbbells for variety.

Reverse Wrist Curl

Muscles worked: Forearms

Exercise type: Single-joint

Movement execution: Take hold of a barbell or strength bar with an overhand grip and your hands three to five inches apart. From there, take a kneeling position perpendicular to the middle of a flat exercise bench and place your forearms over the bench with your hands hanging just off the edge. Keeping your body stationary, proceed to lower your hands as far as you can and, at the bottom, reverse direction and bring the resistance back up as high as possible.

Training tips and variations: As with conventional wrist curls, reverse wrist curls can be executed with dumbbells for variety.

Wrist Roller

Muscles worked: Forearms

Exercise type: Single-joint

Movement execution: Stand with your arms extended directly in front of you holding the ends of a wrist roller with an overhand grip. With the weight hanging down and the line taut, proceed to roll the weight up using the strength in your forearms and wrists. When the resistance reaches the top, slowly unroll the line and repeat.

Training tips and variations: For variety, you can hold the wrist roller with an underhand grip similar to the hand position for conventional wrist curls.

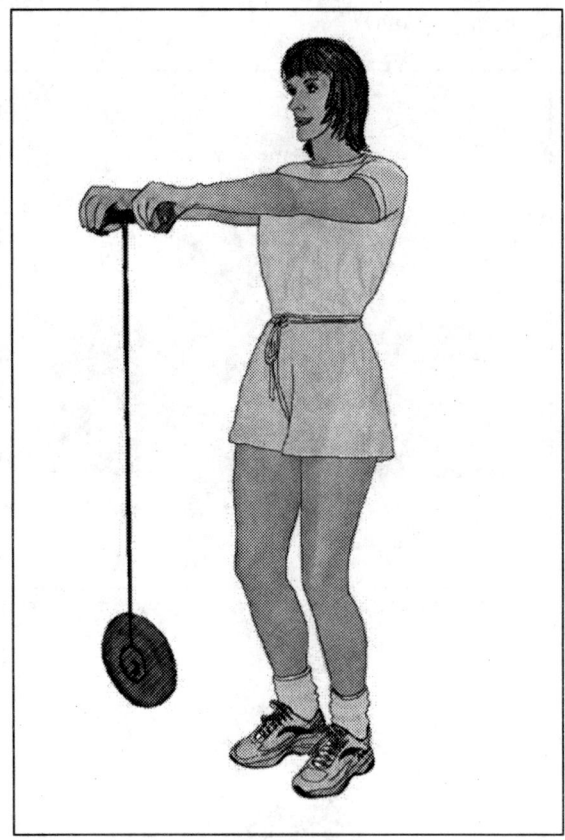

Softball Shoulder Series

While numerous shoulder exercises were detailed previously in Chapter 8, the movements explained next are specifically designed to keep the rotator cuff muscles strong, balanced, and injury free. Regardless of how strong and developed the larger muscles of the shoulders are, weak rotators will hinder joint stability, thus inhibit the performance of the shoulders and arms on the softball field and in the weight room.

The softball shoulder series should be performed at least two days per week on a year-round basis, with the only exception being during the preparation phase of your strength program when core, medicine ball, and body weight movements will be featured. For best results, run through each movement one after the other with minimal rest between sets (20 seconds). Beginners should start with one full circuit and increase the number of circuits as they advance. Experienced trainers should perform three circuits every rotator cuff workout. These exercises will be executed with light dumbbells (2 to 10 lbs. depending on your strength level) and incorporated toward the end of your strength sessions.

Internal Rotation

Muscles worked: Rotator cuff

Exercise type: Single joint

Movement execution: Lie sideways on a flat exercise bench and take hold of an appropriately weighted dumbbell with your lower hand. Keeping your arm bent at a 90-degree angle, rotate it inward to your lower chest area. Return to the low position and repeat.

Training tips and variations: This exercise can also be performed with an elastic band from a standing position.

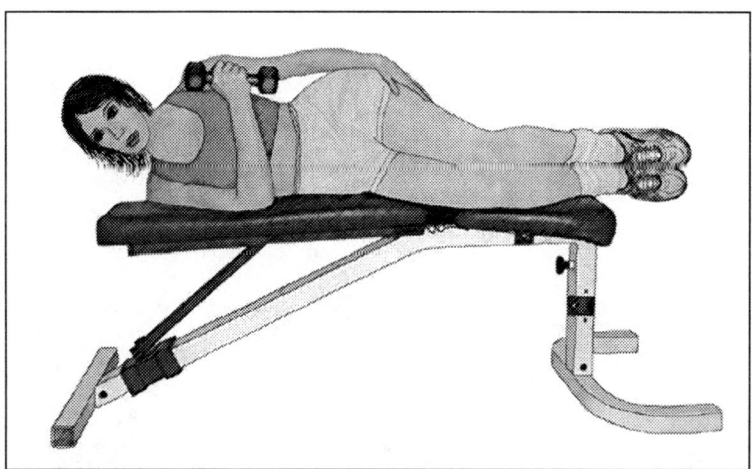

External Rotation

Muscles worked: Rotator cuff

Exercise type: Single-joint

Movement execution: Lie sideways on a flat exercise bench and take hold of an appropriately weighted dumbbell in your upper hand. Keeping your arm bent at a 90-degree angle and your elbow tucked to your upper hip area, rotate it upward. Return to the starting position and repeat.

Training tips and variations: This exercise can also be performed with an elastic band from a standing position.

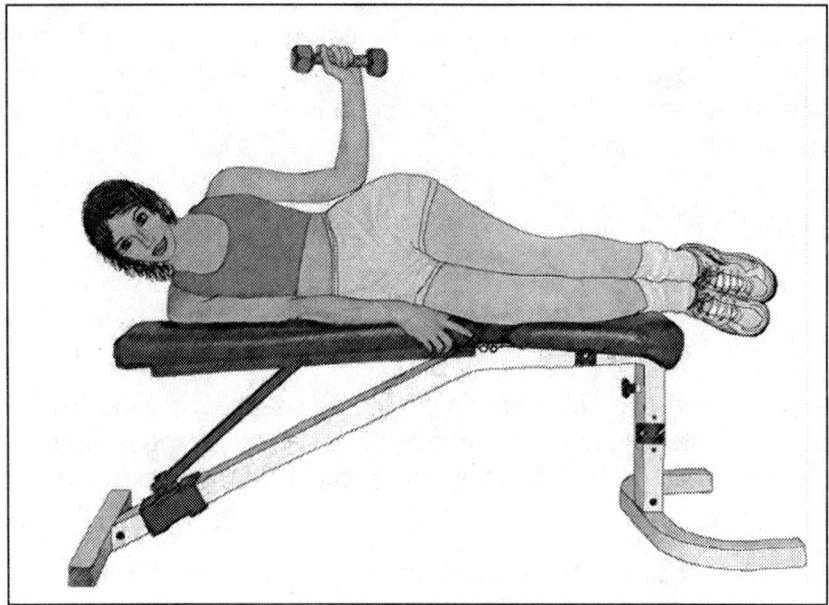

Empty Can

Muscles worked: Rotator cuff

Exercise type: Single-joint

Movement execution: Standing, hold two light dumbbells in your hands with your thumbs facing the floor. Keeping your arms straight, proceed to raise the dumbbells forward and slightly out to each side until each arm is at eye level. Hold for a four count, and then return the resistance to the starting position.

Training tips and variations: This exercise can be performed seated as well as standing.

Hands Up

Muscles worked: Rotator cuff

Exercise type: Single-joint

Movement execution: Stand with an appropriately weighted dumbbell in each hand and hold both arms straight out at approximately shoulder height. Proceed to bend each elbow to 90 degrees so that both hands are pointing toward the floor. From there, rotate both arms upward, while maintaining the elbows at 90 degrees.

Training tips and variations: This movement can be executed seated on the end of a flat exercise bench as well as standing.

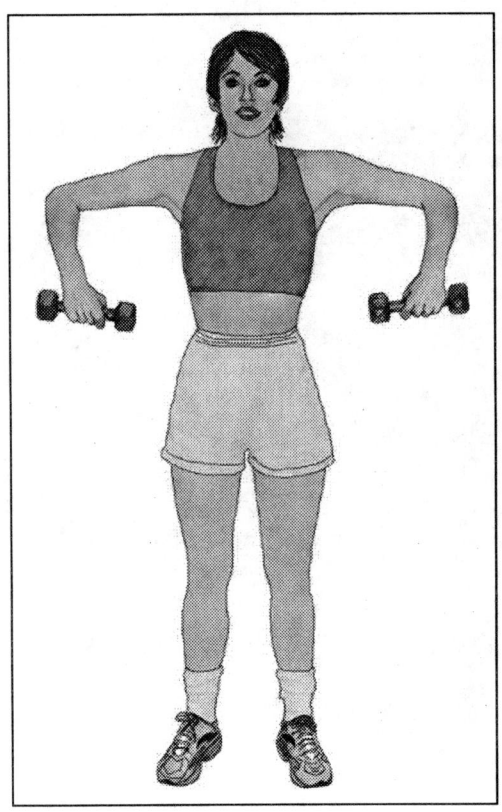 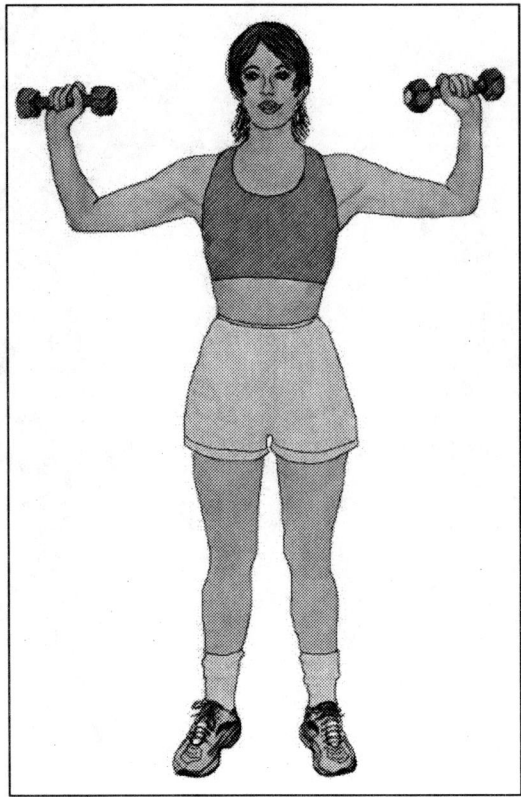

Shoulder Extension

Muscles worked: Rotator cuffs

Exercise type: Single-joint

Movement execution: Grab two appropriately weighted dumbbells and stand with your knees slightly flexed and your upper torso leaning over until it is parallel to the ground. Bring your arms straight back behind you with your thumbs out and palms down until they are even with your upper torso (parallel to the floor). Hold for a two count at the top and return to the starting position.

Training tips and variations: This exercise can be performed with two ground based pulleys for variety.

Bench Dip

Muscles worked: Triceps, entire shoulder girdle, and lower chest

Exercise type: Multi-joint

Movement execution: Sit in the middle of an exercise bench with your hands at your sides and your legs extended in front of you. While balancing on your heels, proceed to lift yourself off the bench and then, by bending at the elbows, lower your body down as far as possible. Once in the low position, pause briefly and then powerfully push yourself up until your arms are fully extended.

Training Tips and variations: To add intensity to this exercise, place a light medicine ball or barbell plate at your midsection during execution.

10

Year-Round Strength Training for Softball

Designing a year-round strength training program for softball is extremely challenging. Tremendous demands come with participating in competitive softball, and finding the time, energy, and motivation to build and maintain strength and power on a year-round basis takes considerable planning and effort.

The basic premise of a softball player's strength program is relatively simple to explain, but very difficult to achieve. Athletes must endeavor to reach peak levels of strength on the initial day of organized practice and maintain that strength over the course of an entire softball season. No easy task to say the least. It is, however, attainable if you conscientiously follow the suggestions and training programs that follow in this chapter.

Year-Round Program

A softball player's yearly strength program will consist of seven separate training cycles, two preparation cycles, four off-season cycles, and one in-season cycle. Cycling is based on incorporating a variety of exercises, weights, set sequences, repetition schemes, and training intensities within a given training year. This proven approach is designed to boost an athlete's strength level in a safe and progressive manner.

The strength workouts will be split as follows: the preparation cycle begins with two weeks of core workouts and is followed by two weeks of sessions that entail both body weight/medicine ball exercises and core movements. The off-season cycles will include three separate workouts, one which focuses on the lower body and total core, another that incorporates upper body and abdominal exercises, and a final session that consists exclusively of combination movements. During the in-season cycle, a variety of full-body workouts with an emphasis on lower body and core exercises will be accomplished. Combination movements, because of their energy draining nature, will not be implemented during the competitive season. Strength workouts should take place on three non-consecutive days per week in both the preparation and off-season cycles. During the in-season cycle, a minimum of two strength training sessions per week should be performed.

Preparation Cycles

Cycle #1

Duration: 2 weeks

Load: Light

Repetition Scheme: 15-50

Objective: This short, two-week cycle focuses on building a base of strength in both the lower back and midsection. As mentioned previously, the core of the body is crucial to not only on-field effectiveness but weight room performance as well. Getting a head start on strengthening these important muscle groups will go a long way toward making your year-round strength program a success. Sample Cycle #1 workouts are detailed in Tables 10-1 and 10-2.

Exercise:	Sets and Repetitions:
Floor Back Raise	4 x 20
Bench Crunch	4 x 50
Good Morning	3 x 15
Straight-Legged Toe Touch	3 x 25
Medicine Ball Twist	2 x 20
Total Sets: 16	

Table 10-1. Sample cycle #1 workout

Exercise:	Sets and Repetitions:
Prone Hyperextension	3 x 15
Medicine Ball Leg Lift	3 x 20
Bicycle Sit-Up	3 x 25
Hip-Up	2 x 20
Total Sets: 14	

Table 10-2. Sample cycle #1 workout

Cycle #2

Duration: 2 weeks

Load: Light

Repetition Scheme: 15-25

Objective: Cycle #2 adds body weight movements and basic medicine ball exercises to the core training you've been performing in Cycle #1. Body weight/low-intensity medicine ball training serve two fundamental purposes. First, it familiarizes you with a form of progressive resistance training that can be accomplished anywhere and at anytime. Many of the body weight and medicine ball exercises you'll be executing in this cycle are just simpler versions of what you'll be doing later on in the weight room.

Second, this type of training will build a base of overall strength that will make your transition to heavier, more intense workouts a smooth one. Body weight, medicine ball, and core workouts will also acclimate the joints to stress, which will help you avoid aches, pains, and injuries later on in your program.

Some experienced trainers may be tempted to skip this short cycle and jump directly to Cycle #3. The thought process being that two extra weeks in the weight room pumping iron will speed up the strength and power development process. Don't make this mistake. Regardless of how much weight training you've done in the past, every strength training year is a new ball game that requires a gradual and progressive approach. This approach is especially true for competitive athletes, most of whom will be coming off a two to four week post-season lay-offs from training before embarking on their off-season strength and conditioning programs. Sample Cycle #2 workouts are detailed in Tables 10-3 through 10-4

Exercise:	Sets and Repetitions:
Wall Slide	3 x 60 seconds
Medicine Ball Push Press	3 x 15
Inverted Chin-Up	3 x 15
Floor Back Raise	3 x 15
Medicine Ball Chest Press	3 x 20
Straight-Legged Toe Touch	4 x 25
Total Sets: 19	

Table 10-3. Sample cycle #2 workout.

Exercise:	Sets and Repetitions:
Body Weight Squat	1 x 20, 2 x 15, 1 x 20
Inverted Chin-Up	3 x 15
Push-Up	3 x 15
Bench Dip	3 x 20
Prone Hyperextension	3 x 15
Medicine Ball Leg Lift	4 x 20
Total Sets: 20	

Table 10-4. Sample cycle #2 workout.

Off-Season Cycles

Cycle #3

Duration: 4 weeks

Load: Light/Medium

Repetition Scheme: 12-15

Objective: This cycle begins your foray into the weight room. The first two weeks of Cycle #3 will be spent learning proper exercise form on all multi-joint and single-joint lifts and becoming generally comfortable in a weight room environment. (A weight room can be an intimating place, especially for a beginner, and it may take awhile for you to feel at home there.) Making a habit of using correct lifting techniques early on in your program will go a long way toward ensuring a successful training year. Remember, bad lifting habits are like comfortable chairs: easy to fall into, hard to get out of.

Once you master correct execution and know your way around the gym, the next step in this cycle involves finding your strength level on all multi-joint movements. This is best accomplished by using a 12-repetition maximum (the weight you can lift 12 times and no more). Once you establish a bench mark in terms of strength, you will use it throughout your program, so try to be as accurate as possible. Sample Cycle #3 workouts are detailed in Tables 10-5 and 10-6.

Exercise:	Sets and Repetitions:
Incline Press	1 x 15, 1 x 12, 1 x 15
Pull-Down	1 x 15, 1 x 12, 1 x 15
DB Shoulder Press	3 x 12
Dip	2 x 12
Bent Lateral Raise	1 x 15, 1 x 12, 1 x 15
Barbell Curl	3 x 15
Medicine Ball Twist	3 x 25
Hanging Leg Raise	3 x 25
Total Sets: 23	

Table 10-5. Sample cycle #3 upper-body workout

Exercise:	Sets and Repetitions:
Leg Press	1 x 15, 2 x 12, 1 x 15
Straight-Legged Dead Lift	3 x 15
Leg Extension	3 x 15
Standing Calf Raise	3 x 15
Prone Hyperextension	3 x 15
Bench Crunch	4 x 25
Total Sets: 20	

Table 10-6. Sample cycle #3 lower-body workout

Cycle #4

Duration: 6 weeks

Load: Medium

Repetition Scheme: 8-12

Objective: By the commencement of Cycle #4 you should be thoroughly familiar with the upper body and lower body movements in your program, as well as with your strength level in all basic, multi-joint lifts. You can now go about the business of developing strength, power, and muscle. Building a solid degree of these three attributes in Cycle #4 will set the stage for the heavy training to come in Cycles #5 and #6. This cycle also introduces you to combination exercises such as push presses, explosive squats, and hang cleans. These complicated movements will be incorporated slowly over a number of workouts, with the emphasis during this phase on learning correct execution and not on testing your strength. Sample Cycle #4 workouts are detailed in Tables 10-7 through 10-9.

Exercise:	Sets and Repetitions:
Chin-Up	1 x 12, 2 x 10, 1 x 12
Bench Press	1 x 12, 2 x 8, 1 x 10
Upright Row	1 x 12, 1 x 10, 1 x 12
Lateral Raise	2 x 12
Lying Triceps Extension	2 x 10
Incline Curl	2 x 12
Medicine Ball Leg Lift	2 x 20
Bicycle Sit-Up	3 x 25
Total Sets: 22	

Table 10-7. Sample cycle #4 upper-body workout

Exercise:	Sets and Repetitions:
Squat	1 x 12, 1 x 10, 1 x 8, 1 x 12
Leg Curl	3 x 12
Lunge	1 x 12, 1 x 10, 1 x 12
Standing Calf Raise	3 x 12
Good Morning	3 x 12
Hanging Leg Raise	4 x 20
Total Sets: 20	

Table 10-8. Sample cycle #4 lower-body workout

Exercise:	Sets and Repetitions:
High Pull	1 x 12, 3 x 8, 1 x 12
Explosive Squat	1 x 12, 3 x 10, 1 x 12
Hang Clean	1 x 12, 1 x 10, 2 x 8, 1 x 12
Total Sets: 15	

Table 10-9. Sample cycle #4 combination workout

Cycle #5

Duration: Six weeks

Load: Medium/Heavy

Repetition Scheme: 6-10

Objective: Intensity is the name of the game in Cycle #5. The goal is substantial strength increases in all lifts (upper body, lower body, and combination). By the end of the cycle, you should be well on your way toward reaching your full-strength and power potential. Although you'll be handling heavier weights throughout Cycle #5, it is still crucial that you maintain proper form on every exercise, set, and repetition. Getting sloppy with execution as weight increases is a tendency. As mentioned previously, improper form, even if it allows you to hoist more weight in the short term, will ultimately stunt your progress, and, more problematic, lead to injury. Sample Cycle #5 workouts are detailed in Tables 10-10 through 10-12.

Exercise:	Sets and Repetitions:
DB Incline Press	1 x 10, 1 x 8, 1 x 6, 1 x 8
DB Row	1 x 10, 2 x 8, 1 x 10
DB Shoulder Press	1 x 8, 1 x 6, 1 x 8
Triceps Press-Down	1 x 10, 1 x 8, 1 x 10
Barbell Curl	1 x 10, 1 x 8, 1 x 10
Straight-Legged Toe Touch	3 x 50
Hip-Up	2 x 50
Total Sets: 22	

Table 10-10. Sample cycle #5 upper-body workout.

Exercise:	Sets and Repetitions:
Step-Up	1 x 10, 1 x 8, 1 x 6, 1 x 8
Straight-Legged Dead Lift	1 x 10, 1 x 8, 1 x 6, 1 x 10
Lunge	3 x 8
Reverse Back Raise	3 x 10
Standing Calf Raise	3 x 10
Bench Crunch	3 x 50
Total Sets: 20	

Table 10-11. Sample cycle #5 lower body workout

Exercise:	Sets and Repetitions:
Push Press	1 x 10, 1 x 8, 2 x 6, 1 x 8
Hang Clean	1 x 10, 1 x 8, 2 x 6, 1 x 10
Explosive Squat	1 x 10, 3 x 8, 1 x 10
Total Sets: 15	

Table 10-12. Sample cycle #5 combination workout

Cycle #6

Duration: Five weeks

Load: Heavy

Repetition Scheme: 4-6

Objective: Cycle #6 will be the culmination of your off-season strength regime. It is also when you'll reach your full potential in the weight room. Combination movements will play a bigger role in this cycle with every other training session being a combination workout. Excitement should be high at this time of year, as the competitive softball season looms ever closer. And, although you won't be spending quite as much time in the weight room as in previous cycles due to skill work and sport-specific conditioning on the softball field, strength gains are still possible and should be the number one objective of Cycle #6. At the conclusion of these five weeks you should be at your strongest in all lifts. Sample Cycle #6 workouts are detailed in Tables 10-13 through 10-15.

Exercise:	Sets and Repetitions:
Pull-Down	1 x 6, 2 x 5, 1 x 6
Bench Press	1 x 6, 2 x 4, 1 x 6
Upright Row	3 x 6
Bent Lateral Raise	2 x 6
DB Curl	2 x 6
Dip	2 x 6
Hanging Leg Raise	3 x 20
Medicine Ball Twist	2 x 25
Total Sets: 22	

Table 10-13. Sample cycle #6 upper body workout.

Exercise:	Sets and Repetitions:
Front Squat	1 x 6, 2 x 4, 1 x 5
Leg Curl	3 x 6
Step-Up	3 x 6
Good Morning	3 x 6
Standing Calf Raise	3 x 6
Medicine Ball Leg Lift	4 x 20
Total Sets: 20	

Table 10-14. Sample cycle #6 lower body workout

Exercise:	Sets and Repetitions:
Hang Clean	1 x 6, 1 x 5, 1 x 4, 1 x 5, 1 x 6
Push Press	4 x 6
High Pull	1 x 6, 1 x 5, 1 x 4, 2 x 6
Total Sets: 14	

Table 10-15. Sample cycle #6 combination workout

In-Season Cycle

Cycle #7

Duration: Throughout the entire competitive softball season

Load: Medium

Repetition scheme: 8-12

Objective: The goal of in-season strength training for softball players can be described in one word: maintenance. Because of games, practices, team meetings, travel, school, along with all of the other obligations and responsibilities in your life, it is virtually impossible to make gains in strength and power during this time of year. But, with a strong commitment and skillful time management, you can preserve the strength you've developed in the off-season. Most softball players become somewhat deconditioned during a long, game-filled season. (Remember, unlike basketball and soccer players, softball athletes get almost no conditioning benefit from participating in their sport.) Adhering to the strength training protocol in this chapter can help you reverse this deconditioning process and enable you to sustain peak levels of strength and performance throughout the competitive season. Sample Cycle #7 workouts are detailed in Tables 10-16 and 10-17.

Exercise:	Sets and Repetitions:
Lunge	1 x 12, 1 x 10, 1 x 12
Straight-Legged Dead Lift	1 x 12, 1 x 10, 1 x 12
Incline Press	1 x 10, 1 x 8, 1 x 10
Chin-Up	1 x 12, 1 x 8, 1 x 12
Lateral Raise	3 x 10
Reverse Back Raise	3 x 12
Straight-Legged Toe Touch	4 x 50
Total Sets: 22	

Table 10-16. Sample cycle #7 full-body workout

Exercise:	Sets and Repetitions:
Squat	1 x 12, 1 x 10, 1 x 8, 1 x 10
Leg Press	2 x 10
Dumbbell Row	1 x 12, 1 x 8, 1 x 12
Dip	1 x 12, 1 x 8, 1 x 10
DB Shoulder Press	1 x 12, 1 x 8, 1 x 10
Machine Back Extension	3 x 12
Bicycle Sit-Up	4 x 25
Total Sets: 22	

Table 10-17. Sample cycle #7 full-body workout

The following examples outline some suggestions that will help you maintain your strength all season long:

- *Make multi-joint exercises the priority*: While combination movements are not prescribed for in-season use by softball players, other multi-joint exercises such as incline presses, squats, and straight legged dead lifts are. These lifts will be the staples of your in-season strength routine. As previously mentioned, using multi-joint exercises is the most energy and time efficient way to strength train, since these movements work numerous muscles at once.

- *Strength train immediately following games*: If you have access to the appropriate facilities, strength training immediately after games is a tremendous way to keep current with your program. Working out subsequent to games also helps cool your body down, allowing you to relax and ultimately sleep more soundly on game nights. Post-game strength workouts should be relatively brief (no longer than 30 minutes or so), and large amounts of hydrating fluids must be consumed before, during, and after the session. It is also imperative that you respect your energy level after competition, especially if you're a pitcher who's just pitched multiple innings, along with monitoring any injuries you may have sustained during the game that would make a post-game strength workout unadvisable.

- *Use off days constructively*: As any competitive athlete can attest, off days during the busy regular season are precious commodities. A free day provides a softball player with an excellent opportunity to hit the weights hard. Strength training consistently on days without games or practices will go a long way toward ensuring that you maintain your strength throughout the season.

- *Schedule a team-strength workout instead of practice*: It is ultimately up to the coach of course, but having a team strength training session, in lieu of practice, can accomplish a great deal. Along with allowing players to stay up to date with their strength programs, it provides everyone—players, coaches, and even team managers—a mental break from the monotony of regular practice.

- *Strength train consistently in the off-season*: Perhaps the best way to ensure that you remain strong and powerful throughout the long softball season is to dedicate yourself to working consistently hard in the weight room during the off-season. The more strength you build in the off-season, the easier it will be to maintain peak performance levels when it counts during the competitive season.

PART IV
MOVEMENT TRAINING FOR SOFTBALL

11

Balance Training

All elite athletes possess great balance. Watch Mia Hamm dribble a soccer ball, Lisa Leslie shoot a basketball, or Annika Sorenstam swing a golf club, and you'll quickly see that balance is essential. All are on balance when performing the skills that their respective sports demand. In fact, you'd be hard pressed to find more than a handful of instances where top athletes, including the ones mentioned above, were caught off balance during competition.

Balance must always precede any forceful movement on the softball field. Regardless of what skill you're executing be it hitting, running, pitching, or fielding, balancing your body properly is mandatory. Therefore, all softball players should make improving their balance a priority.

While balance has always been recognized as important for athletes, balance training was relatively slow to come to the sports world. As strength and conditioning has evolved, however, direct balance work has become a prerequisite for all improvement conscious athletes. Through the hard work of creative trainers and conditioning specialists, numerous specifically designed balance exercises exist that you can incorporate into your conditioning program. Performing these exercises regularly will enhance your balance considerably and go a long way toward making you a better softball player. Many helpful balance exercises are described later in this chapter.

Equipment

- *Athletic tape*: Tape is used for line touch drills. Any type of athletic tape will suffice as long as the color contrasts with the training surface.

- *Medicine balls*: Medicine balls were discussed earlier in the strength training section. For balance drills, the weight of the ball will vary depending on your strength, athletic ability, and the particular exercises involved. Most softball players will work with medicine balls that weigh between two and five kilograms.

- *Balance pad*: A balance pad is simply a foam mat that causes an athlete's feet to sink into the cushion, thus creating instability.

- *Balance board*: A variety of balance boards are available for your use. Most consist of a single platform with a fulcrum (or fulcrums) underneath that creates an unstable environment, forcing an athlete to constantly adjust to maintain balance. Some newer balance boards move in three axes for greater instability. You can perform numerous balance exercises while standing on this equipment, including the ones detailed as follows.

- *Footwear*: Many strength and conditioning specialists feel that balance training, especially when undertaken on a balance pad or balance board, should be accomplished barefoot. Not wearing footwear will help to strengthen your feet and ankles to a greater degree. Of course, if you're training on a rough surface or have any type of lower leg or foot injury, wearing basketball sneakers or cross training shoes during balance workouts is recommended.

Parameters of Balance Training

All balance exercises in the following program will be performed unilaterally (on one leg). The exercises progress from simple (single-leg stands) to advanced (one legged side toss and catch). The movements should be executed in a smooth, controlled style while standing on the ball of your foot. Training balance in a jerky-jerky manner or from a flatfooted position defeats the purpose.

Be aware that many of the balance exercises detailed as follows are much more difficult than they appear. It is important that you don't get frustrated. Even the most gifted athletes usually struggle with these movements during the first few workouts. With time, improvements in exercise execution and overall balance will come.

Schedule Description

Program Length

A balance-training program for softball should be a year-round endeavor, with the exception of training breaks where complete abstinence from exercise is scheduled. Because of the low, non-impact feature, balance training is not taxing on the body. Therefore, training balance on a year-round basis is not only possible but encouraged.

Number of Workouts Per Week

Three balance workouts per week are suggested in the off-season. During the competitive season, two balance workouts should be accomplished.

Sets and Repetitions

Eight to twelve total sets per workout are recommended for balance training. One set in balance-training terminology will include performing the exercise on each leg. Usually, sets will be spread between three to five different exercises. The repetition range per set will generally be between 10 to 15 for each leg.

Rest between Sets

The rest between sets of balance exercises will vary between 30 to 90 seconds depending on the intensity of the effort and the fitness level of the athlete.

Workout Duration

Most balance workouts can be completed in less than 20 minutes.

Balance Exercises

- *Single-leg stands*: This simple exercise entails standing erect on one leg with your knee slightly flexed for 30 to 60 seconds. The raised leg should be bent at the knee and positioned behind your body parallel to the floor. To increase difficulty, try this exercise with your eyes closed. Single-leg stands are best performed on a soft surface such as a balance pad.

- *Curb walks*. Curb walks can be executed on any slim curb (four to eight inches wide). The exercise resembles what a gymnast would do on a balance beam—minus the flips and cartwheels of course. Once you locate an appropriately sized curb, proceed to step one foot in front of the other without falling off the curb. The distance of the walk can vary from a few steps to 10 yards depending on your proficiency and the length of the curb. This drill not only improves balance, but will help you enhance your powers of concentration as well; one small lapse of attention can easily result in a loss of balance and a fall off the curb. Unless you have a background in gymnastics, don't try this on a regulation balance beam, which is usually four or five feet above the ground. Falling from that height is not a pleasant experience, as you can imagine. To increase the difficulty of this exercise, you can carry light dumbbells in each hand during execution.

- *Line touches*: Place a strip of athletic tape on the floor in front of you. Stand on one leg where the tape begins and, with your back straight, proceed to bend at the hips, knee, and ankle, reaching as far as you can with the hand of the raised leg and touch the tape. Continue for the required number of repetitions then repeat standing on the opposite leg. Make sure to mark you results from week to week to check progress.

- *Medicine ball pick-ups*: Place an appropriately weighted medicine ball approximately a foot in front of you. Begin by standing on one leg with your knee slightly flexed. Then, bend forward at the hips, knee, and ankle and with both hands grab the ball from the floor and rise up to the standing position. You can either bring the ball up to your midsection or, to increase difficulty, raise it overhead. After completing the

Curb walks

Line touches

repetition, hand the ball to a coach or training partner and have her place it back on the floor. Continue for the required number of repetitions. Switch standing legs and repeat. To increase difficulty, place the ball farther out in front of you and/or try executing the exercise on an unstable surface such as a balance pad or balance board.

- *Around the worlds*: Standing on your right leg with your hips, knee, and ankle slightly flexed, move either a volleyball, basketball, or medicine ball as fast as possible under your knee from right to left, then around your back from left to right. Reverse course (right to left around your back; left to right under your knee) and continue in this pattern for the required number of repetitions. Stand on your left leg and repeat the action. To increase difficulty, try performing this exercise on an unstable surface such as a balance pad or balance board.

- *One-legged side toss and catch*: Stand on one leg with your grounded knee slightly flexed. Your raised leg should be bent at the knee and placed behind your body parallel to the ground. Begin by twisting your torso as far as you can to the left while keeping your grounded leg stationary and receive a medicine ball pass from your training partner who will be standing six to eight feet away off your left shoulder. Once you catch the pass, immediately position the ball just above waist height, 8 to 12 inches from your body. From there, twist your torso as far as possible to your right, keeping your arms and grounded leg stationary. Then in a controlled but powerful

Medicine ball pick-ups

Around the worlds

manner, swing back in the opposite direction and release the ball just after it crosses the middle of your body to your training partner. Continue for the required number of repetitions. Do the same while standing on the opposite leg. To increase difficulty, try this exercise while standing on an unstable surface such as a balance pad or balance board. Less advanced athletes should use a basketball or softball for this drill in lieu of a medicine ball.

One-legged side toss and catch

Exercise:	Sets and Repetitions:
Single-Leg Stands	2 x 60 seconds
Line Touches	2 x 15
Around the Worlds	2 x 10
Medicine Ball Pick-Ups	1 x 12, 1 x 15, 1 x 12
One-Legged Side Toss and Catch	1 x 12, 1 x 15, 1 x 12

Table 11-1. Sample balance workout

12

Speed Training

Straight ahead running speed is extremely important in softball. Just some of the instances in which you run all-out from point A to point B on the softball field include running to first base on a bunt or ground ball, flagging down a fly ball in the outfield gap, stealing a base, and chasing after a passed ball or wild pitch that is bouncing toward the backstop.

The first six to eight strides of a sprint are most important for softball athletes. Improving your acceleration, which is the ability to reach maximum speed in the shortest amount of time, will therefore be the main objective of your speed training program. While possessing and developing a high top speed, such as the kind you incorporate in the final 30 yards of a 60-yard sprint, is certainly beneficial, but for softball performance purposes acceleration is the key. Think about it. The average distance traversed by a fielder in a softball game at one time is five to 10 feet, with even centerfielders rarely running more than 10 yards after a batted ball. On offense, sprinting to first occurs frequently, but the bag is just 40 feet from home plate, which if you account for overrunning first base only entails running 45 feet or so. Legging out a double or running from first to third is less common and would cause you to sprint approximately 80 feet. The rare triple demands about a 120-foot run, still only 40 yards.

Three Paths for Increasing Sprinting Speed

For decades the advice from the "experts" concerning increasing sprinting speed was simple, "don't waste your time". Fast runners were born and not made they said, and athletes were better off spending training time working on improving the skills of their particular sport rather than trying in vain to increase their running speed. Recent findings, however, have proved this way of thinking quite erroneous. Athletes in a variety of sports, including softball, have substantially improved their sprinting speed through proper training.

The following information will provide the necessary tools to enhance your ability to run fast. It is then up to you to put in the requisite effort and proceed to apply your newfound speed on the softball field.

Conditioning

If you hope to reach your full potential in terms of sprinting speed, it is imperative that you first acquire a high level of physical conditioning. Being both aerobically and anaerobically fit, as well as achieving your optimal body weight, is required.

Good cardiovascular fitness will allow you to train consistently hard, which is an absolute necessity if you're to tolerate and get the most out of your speed workouts. Speed training is very demanding, and if your body is not up to the physical task, speed increases will not take place.

Realizing your ideal body weight speaks for itself. Not too many overweight athletes run fast. And if they do, they could surely run quite a bit faster if a proper body weight was maintained. Carrying too much weight on your frame also increases the risk of sustaining a lower body injury during your speed training sessions.

It is not necessary that we go further into detail about specific conditioning methods here—the rest of the book does that—but just remain aware that in order to run as fast as your genetic capability allows, attaining top shape is the first step.

Athletic Ability

Athletic ability has many definitions. For the purposes of this chapter, athletic ability will refer to the attributes of quickness, agility, flexibility, strength, balance, and explosive power. Improving these aspects will help you run faster. The quicker and more agile you are, the faster you'll reach your maximum speed (acceleration). As mentioned previously, acceleration is the most important type of speed for softball players. The more flexible your muscles, the better they will respond when sprinting, especially when it comes to increasing stride length, an important factor in how fast you run. (Stride length is discussed in the next section on running mechanics.) A stronger lower body will enable you to generate more force off the ground during your stride cycle, thus translating into more speed. Improving upper body strength also contributes to increased running speed by allowing for more powerful arm motion. The better balanced runner will be the more efficient runner. Increased efficiency equals faster sprinting. Explosiveness training such as plyometrics promotes forceful muscular contractions, which lead to faster movement.

The great news concerning all the athletic attributes mentioned is that they can be improved significantly by following the training programs and suggestions in *Peak Conditioning Training for Softball*. Focused work on enhancing your athletic ability will pay great dividends when you hit the track, field, or hills for your speed workouts, not to mention when you're breaking up that inning-extending double play at second or sprinting home from third with the winning run after tagging up on a fly ball.

Running Mechanics

An important variable in increasing sprinting speed involves improving your running mechanics. Although every individual athlete has a unique running style, you can implement numerous fundamental sprint-enhancing techniques that will help you reach your ultimate speed potential.

The two major factors in how fast you run can be described in a simple equation: stride length x stride frequency = running speed. Stride length is the space covered in an individual stride. Stride frequency is the time it takes to accomplish a single stride. To become a faster sprinter, you must enhance your stride length by intensifying the force against the ground, while maintaining balance with your stride frequency. Powerful and efficient arm movement also must be employed. The following list details the characteristics of effective sprinting:

- During your first few strides from a stationary position, it is important that you stay low. Standing up too quickly at the onset of a run will slow you down.

- Once you cover the first few yards of any sprint, running in a naturally erect position is central to good sprinting technique. Many young athletes have been erroneously taught to lean forward when sprinting. This positioning will actually slow you down and can contribute to a lost of balance at high speeds.

- Your head should be up and straight, with your eyes focused toward the destination of the run.

- Your arms, shoulders, and hands should be relaxed when sprinting. Many athletes have a tendency to keep their upper bodies rigid when running at top speed. Remember, in order to reach your sprinting potential, you must always remain relaxed.

- Your push-off leg should always end up completely extended, and it's important not to overstride during your stride cycle. Increasing your stride length in an unnatural fashion by forcing your lead foot to land far ahead of your body will hinder your sprinting speed.

- Arm action should always come from your shoulders when sprinting. During the upswing, your hands should reach just in front of your chin and slightly inside your shoulders. On the downswing, your hands should reach no further back than your hips.

- Artificially increasing your stride frequency by attempting to move your legs too quickly will make you move fast but mostly in one place—not very helpful when it comes to beating out an infield hit. Traversing the maximum amount of ground in the shortest period of time involves the correct balance of stride frequency and stride length.

- Your elbows should always be kept at a 90-degree angle, forcing all arm action to stay close to the body. If your arms are too far from your torso when sprinting, it will, more times than not, disrupt the rhythm of your stride.

- Your torso should remain mostly stationary when sprinting, with the shoulders squared to your destination.

Like all athletic skills, sprinting properly requires repetitive practice. Aspire to follow these guidelines during your anaerobic conditioning workouts that include running and when executing softball specific skills such as base running and outfield practice. Additionally, if you have the opportunity, seek out an experienced track coach to help you perfect your running form. Most high school and college programs have knowledgeable track coaches on staff who are usually more than happy to share their expertise. (They may, however, try to recruit you for the track team!) Some athletes may consider hiring a personal running coach. If you decide to go this route, which probably will be expensive, just make sure that the trainer's credentials are legitimate.

Specialized Drills and Techniques for Enhancing Speed

Similar to your quickness/agility program (Chapter 13), you will incorporate three different types of drills in your speed workouts: speed technique drills, resistance sprinting, and overspeed training. Next, all three are discussed in detail, along with their attendant drills.

Speed Technique Drills

Speed technique drills, as the name suggests, are designed to improve your running mechanics. The drills range in intensity from very light (arm swings) to high (acceleration sprints). In order to get the most out of speed technique drills you must remain mindful of your running form. Eventually your mind and body will synchronize, allowing proper running form to come about naturally without conscious effort.

Drill: Arm Swings

Execution: Stand with your knees slightly bent and your legs shoulder-width apart. Proceed to swing your arms repetitively as if you were sprinting.

Drill : Up and Downs

Execution: Standing with a straight posture, attempt to lift one knee as high as possible while keeping the other leg planted firmly on the ground. Alternate legs each repetition. Your arms should swing up and down naturally, as if you were running in place.

Drill: Form Strides

Execution: Stride at a medium, even pace over the course of a run, always focusing on form rather than speed. Form strides are best performed at distances between 50 and 200 meters.

Drill: Ladder Runs

Execution: Spread a speed ladder out over a soft, even running surface. The ladder itself will consist of 10 to 12 rungs, which have graduated spacing from shortest to longest. Proceed to sprint explosively in between each rung.

Working out with the speed ladder forces you to take short, quick steps at the beginning of a sprint, discouraging the common problem of over striding and allowing you to accelerate at a faster pace. As mentioned earlier in the chapter, the first six to eight strides are most important for softball performance. Ladder runs will help you increase your speed over these crucial initial strides.

Drill: Acceleration Sprints

Execution: Begin by running at a slow pace and proceed by gradually increasing your speed over the course of the run until you're at top speed. For example, if you were engaging in a 100-meter acceleration sprint, you would commence by jogging about 15 meters, accelerate for 40 meters or so, and then ramp up to an all out sprint for the duration of the run.

Added Resistance Sprinting

As the name suggests, added resistance sprinting calls for adding weight or resistance to your frame in order to make the act of sprinting more difficult. You can accomplish this in a number of ways. The following are some of the most popular:

• *Uphill sprinting*: Uphill sprinting is a tried and true method of training that increases running speed. Athletes in a variety of sports from basketball to soccer include this technique in their workout regimes. And, unlike many other added resistence sprinting techniques, it will cost you nothing in terms of fancy equipment. The only requirement is an appropriate running landscape.

The hill grade you incorporate for your uphill sprint workouts will vary depending on your goals and individual conditioning level. As a rule, steep grades (7 to 10-degree angles) should be utilized for short, explosive runs covering 5 to 15 yards or so. Flatter grades (1.5 to 3.5-degree angles) should be used for longer runs (25 to 80 yards). A weighted vest or any other additional form of resistance should not be incorporated for uphill sprints. The hills will provide enough resistance.

• *Weighted-vest sprinting*: Sprinting while wearing a weighted vest has shown to be an effective way to increase running speed. However, if executed improperly, it can also be dangerous. The correct (and safe) way to incorporate a weighted vest in your speed development program is discussed as follows.

The weight of the vest should never be heavier than 8 to 10 percent of your body weight. A higher ratio of vest weight to body weight will increase the risk of impact related injury substantially.

Weight should be added to the vest gradually from workout to workout as strength, conditioning, and speed improve. Even elite athletes follow this protocol, sometimes taking a half-dozen weighted vest sprint workouts before the aforementioned vest-weight-to-body-weight ratio is reached.

It is imperative that proper and natural running form be maintained at all times during weighted-vest sprint workouts. If the weight of the vest interferes with your running form, the vest is too heavy. It is always better to perform these training sessions with less weight, rather than compromising form and risking injury by pushing it.

If you suffer from lower back or knee problems, running with a weighted vest is not recommended. The additional weight, even if it's only a small percentage of your body weight, can easily exacerbate these conditions.

• *Two-person harness*: The two-person harness is used frequently by track athletes and football wide receivers to improve their acceleration. Training with this equipment entails having one partner hold the handles and attempt not to give ground while the other partner sprints straight ahead, pulling the resistance to the best of her ability. It helps if your partner is approximately the same weight as you for obvious reasons.

Two-person harness training is a tremendous vehicle for improving short-distance (3 to 10 yards) acceleration, which is extremely important for softball players. Therefore, this type of added resistance training should be featured in all softball speed enhancement programs.

• *Resistance parachute*: Sales of resistance parachutes have skyrocketed in recent years as more and more athletes of all ages aspire to increase their ability run fast. While much of the equipment's popularity stems from its high-tech look, parachutes, if designed properly and used correctly, provide speed training benefits.

The parachute is attached to the body by a waist strap. The idea is to accelerate gradually into a full sprint, allowing the chute to catch the wind and make the run more difficult. Some parachutes come with a quick release feature that allows for mid-stride release, thus promoting a sudden burst of speed that can increase stride frequency. Resistance parachute workouts should be accomplished on a running track or on even, low-cut grass.

The biggest disadvantage of the resistance parachute is durability. They are known to tangle, not open, and rip during workouts. Purchasing the parachute from a reliable manufacturer gives you the best chance to avoid these problems.

• *Water Sprinting*: As mentioned previously, water workouts have become extremely popular in the world of sports training. For speed enhancement purposes, water provides natural resistance, thus running in a pool is a terrific low-impact way to get a productive sprint workout. Water treadmills are also available for use at many health clubs, fitness centers, and university athletic facilities. This equipment allows you to run on a submerged footpad against water current that can be adjusted to suit your needs. Needless to say, this workout is a great speed and conditioning training tool for injured athletes who are not quite ready for ground pounding.

• *Sled pulls*: Resistance sleds are used frequently by football players and are actually modeled after the old-fashion blocking sleds you see on most football practice fields. The difference, of course, is that blocking sleds are pushed and resistance sleds are pulled.

These low-tech apparatus, when used correctly, provide solid speed and lower body power improvements in athletes. You simply adjust the weight of the sled (usually by adding or subtracting barbell plates), attach the shoulder/waist harness to your torso, and off you go.

Two of the keys to productive sled pull workouts include staying low and driving forward explosively throughout each and every sprint. Rising up will cause you to lose your momentum, which will slow you down and ultimately hinder your speed development. Additionally, it is imperative that you locate an even stretch of low-cut grass for sled pulls. Uneven terrain makes movement of the sled and your body awkward and can increase the risk of injury.

Overspeed Training

Overspeed training enhances your ability to run fast by increasing your stride length and rate. Similar to plyometrics (Chapter 14), this type of workout forces your neuromuscular system to become accustomed to faster speeds and, therefore, enables you to attain those speeds without facilitation. Overspeed training is very intense and demands complete concentration and a high level of physical conditioning.

• *Downhill sprinting*: Downhill sprinting was perhaps the first form of overspeed training ever developed. And, it continues to be great way to entice your legs to move faster. (If they don't, a roll down the hill could be in your future.) The execution simply entails sprinting at full speed with your body balanced and under control down an appropriately steep hill. The downgrade of the hill should be approximately three degrees. Anything steeper is not advisable, because it will compromise running form and may be dangerous. The length of the downhill stretch for softball training purposes should range from 10 to 40 yards. Even more so than other running drills, downhill sprinting requires that you be fully stretched and warm prior to execution.

• *Follow the leader*: This form of overspeed training is more psychological than physiological. Start by giving your training partner a 5 to 10 foot head start in a sprint race. Then try to catch up with her over the course of the run. The distance of the sprint can vary anywhere from 20 to 60 yards or longer depending on your training objectives.

The follow the leader drill is less demanding from a physical standpoint than that of other overspeed methods. However, because of the pride/competition component (the determination to catch or at least gain ground on your partner), it has shown to be a fun and productive way for athletes to improve their sprinting speed.

• *Towing*: Towing has shown to be an effective form of overspeed training. Many athletes in a variety of sports where speed is important incorporate this method regularly. It works like this: attach the towing apparatus, which consists of strong elastic tubing and a waist belt, to your body and to a training partner or secure object such as a football goal post or backstop.  Proceed to walk backwards facing the partner/secure object where the tubing is attached approximately 30 meters. Pause briefly and begin to sprint all-out as the tubing snaps back and pulls you forward.

Towing workouts should always be executed on soft, even surfaces. Well-manicured football/soccer fields are best. Soft terrain is a must for theses sessions, as spills are commonplace. It is also very important that proper running form is maintained during towing sprints. Most well-made elastic tubing will stretch five to six times its relaxed length. For safety reasons, check the tubing carefully for any damage prior to all towing workouts.

13

Quickness and Agility Training

Quickness and agility are coveted attributes on the softball field. Players who possess these qualities have the ability to react immediately and explosively from stationary positions, change direction on a dime with little or no modulation of speed, and accelerate quickly while running straight ahead, sliding laterally, or backpedaling.

As your quickness and agility improve, so will many of your softball skills. Just a few improvements include bounding off the mound to field a bunt, exploding out of the batter's box toward first base, breaking on a line drive hit to the outfield, getting a jump enroute to a stolen base, and sliding into position on balls hit to the infield. Many other positive byproducts come with increased quickness and agility, but those mentioned should be enough to encourage you to work hard on improving this facet of your game.

Schedule Description

Quickness/agility training should be engaged on a year-round basis. In the off-season, three quickness/agility workouts per week are suggested. These sessions are best combined with either your speed or plyometric workouts, as all three training disciplines are similar in terms of physical demands.

Once organized practice begins in the spring, two quickness/agility workouts per week will suffice. The majority of these sessions will take place prior to practices and games. Off days may also be used when appropriate.

Keeping up with this quickness/agility training during the season is especially important for softball athletes. Unlike in a sport like basketball where actually playing the game provides a good deal of quickness/agility work, softball competitions offer very little in the way of repetitive, quick movement, certainly not enough to garner a solid workout. Therefore, while athletes in sports such as soccer, basketball, volleyball, etc., will require very little in the way of direct quickness/agility training during their seasons, softball players must maintain regular quickness/agility workouts throughout the competitive campaign.

Quickness/agility workouts can be performed in a variety of settings. Some appropriate locations include a gymnasium with wood flooring (a great venue because basketball courts provide floor lines that can be incorporated as markers), rubberized running tracks, hard-packed sand, and, of course, any manicured softball outfield. Hard surfaces, such as pavement and blacktop, and any type of uneven terrain should be avoided for quickness/agility training.

High intensity is the key to any successful quickness/agility program. After completing your warm-up, all drills should be undertaken at full speed. No exceptions exist for this training. The only way to get the most out of your quickness/agility program is to go full throttle for the duration of each and every drill. Remember, high intensity training equals increased quickness and agility. Table 13-1 presents an overview of the basic parameters for conducting quickness/agility training.

Program length:	Year-round
Drill duration:	15 to 30 seconds
Drills per workout:	3 to 4
Rest intervals:	30 to 60 seconds
Sets:	10 to 20
Intensity:	Very high

Table 13-1. Recommended parameters for quickness/agility training

Quickness/Agility Drills

Your softball quickness/agility program will consist of three different types of drills. The first kind, quick movement drills, entails a series of short distance hops that encourage you to get your feet moving as fast as possible. Specific movement pattern drills are next. They will help you to perfect the functional movement patterns and footwork required in softball. The final type, random movement pattern drills, are most challenging and will advance your ability to change direction quickly, start and stop efficiently, react to situations, as well as improving your hand-eye coordination.

Quick Movement Drills

Drill: Front Line Hops

Execution: Stand facing the foul line with your feet close together. On command, hop back and forth over the line as fast as possible. Continue for the required time.

Drill: Lateral Line Hops

Execution: Stand parallel to the foul line with your feet close together. On command, hop back and forth laterally over the line as fast as possible. Continued for the required time.

Drill: Four Way Box Hops

Execution: Place two pieces of athletic tape in a box shape in front of you. Proceed to hop as quickly as possible from one quadrant to another for the required time.

Drill: One Leg Hop Series

Execution: The one leg hop series entails performing all the previous drills on one leg. One leg quick movement drills, as you might imagine, are more difficult than the two-leg variety. Incorporate them gradually into your routine as your strength, balance, quickness, and agility improve.

Specific Movement Pattern Drills

Drill: Side Shuffle

Execution: Start in an athletic ready stance (on the balls of your feet, knees comfortable flexed, feet at shoulder width, back taut, and head straight) and proceed to side shuffle (slide sideways without crossing your feet) back and forth over an eight-yard course for the required time.

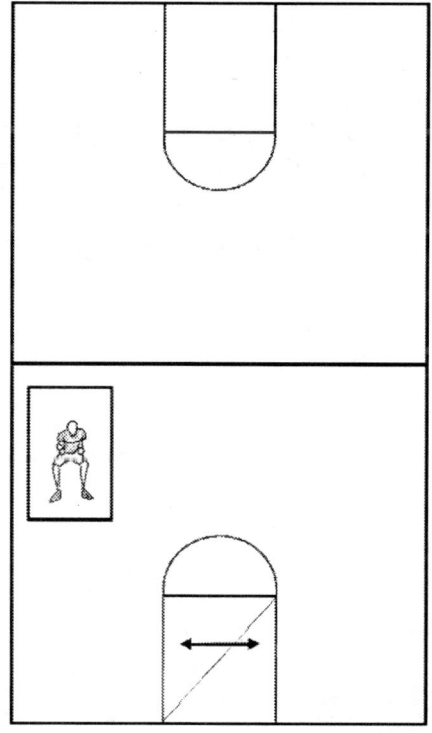

Drill: Sprint, Side Shuffle, Backpedal

Execution: Assume an athletic stance on an open field or court. On command, sprint eight yards straight ahead. Then, proceed to side shuffle five yards to your left. From there, immediately backpedal for eight yards. Continue for the required time. Repeat the pattern, but this time side shuffle to your right instead of your left.

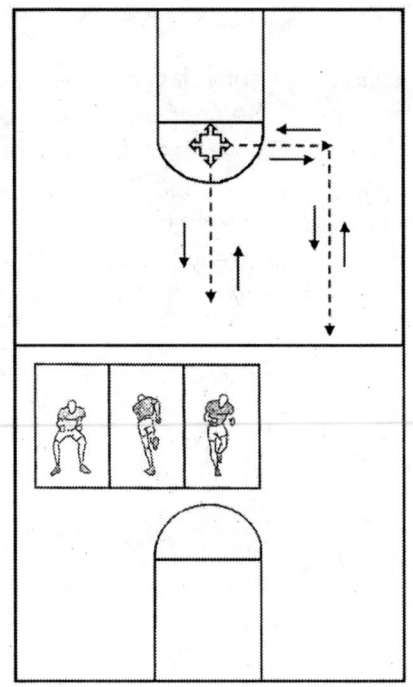

Drill: Mini-Cone Shuffle

Execution: Place a series of mini-cones or other low-lying barriers a foot or so apart. Using small side steps, shuffle over the cones without crossing your feet, always concentrating on spending as little time as possible on the ground. When you get to the end of the row, reverse course and repeat back and forth for the required time.

Drill: In and Outs

Execution: Standing parallel to the front of a speed latter, step in the first rung with your outside foot. Once your outside foot lands, immediately step in the same rung with your inside foot. After your inside foot lands, continue by stepping outside the ladder with your outside foot. Follow immediately by stepping outside the ladder with your inside foot. Proceed in the same pattern to the end of the ladder. Once you reach the end of the ladder, reverse course and repeat the pattern.

Random Movement Pattern Drills

Drill: Side Shuffle with Response

Execution: Start in athletic ready stance. Have a coach or training partner shout move and proceed to side shuffle left or right. When your coach/training partner shouts again, change direction quickly and side shuffle the opposite way. Continue to side shuffle back and forth on response for the required time.

Drill: Change Direction with Response

Execution: Assume an athletic stance. Have your coach or training partner stand facing you approximately 15 feet away. Respond to your coach/training partner's direction to either side shuffle left or right, backpedal, or sprint straight ahead. Continue for the required time.

Drill: Bean Bag Pass and Catch

Execution: Stand facing a partner six to eight feet apart, each holding a small beanbag in one hand. (A tennis or squash ball can be substituted for the beanbag.) Proceed to side shuffle across the field or court while softly tossing the balls back and forth. As you become proficient at the drill, begin to incorporate more difficult throws (in front, behind, high, low, etc.) to your partner. Continue for the required time.

Drill: Reaction Belt Response Drill

Execution: To start, both you and your partner will fasten a five-foot, Velcro reaction belt to your waists. Your partner will then proceed in no set pattern to make a series of quick, unpredictable movements and you should attempt to follow as close as possible. The objective is to keep the belt on as long as you can without it breaking free, preferably for the duration of the drill. To get the most out of the drill, try to engage a partner who is quicker and more agile than you are.

Drill: Reaction Ball Chase

Execution: Assume an athletic stance facing a coach or training partner. Then, have the coach/training partner drop or toss a reaction ball (a small, ridged ball that bounces in unpredictable fashion) five to eight feet in front of you. Proceed to chase the ball down, pick it up, and return it to your coach/training partner. Repeat for the required number of repetitions.

14

Plyometrics

Plyometrics, or "jump training" as it was originally termed in Europe, is a form of training that involves a series of jumps, hops, bounds, and medicine ball throws that link speed with strength to produce power. This power is achieved by stretching or loading the muscles as fast as possible prior to a forceful contraction. Perhaps the best way to understand how plyometrics works is to think of your muscles as rubber bands stretched to capacity then abruptly released, allowing the force and energy to move explosively in the opposite direction.

While one of the main byproducts of plyometric training, improving vertical jump, is not a high priority for softball players, the ability to produce explosive power is of great use on the softball field. Increasing your explosive power will substantially improve your ability to run, throw, pitch, and hit.

Developing a Plyometric Program for Softball

A number of factors should be taken into account when designing a plyometric program for softball, including the following.

Equipment

Although many plyometric drills can be executed without equipment, you should be familiar with the accessories detailed as follows:

- *Barriers*: Barriers are incorporated into many plyometric drills. Their height will vary from as low as six inches to as high as two feet or more, depending on the nature of the drill and the athletic ability of the practitioner. The safest barriers are made of foam padding. The simplest and most widely used are plastic cones. Obviously, hard objects should never be used as a plyometric barrier.

- *Boxes*: Boxes used for plyometrics should be sturdy; have semi-soft, non-slip landing surfaces; and can range from one foot to over three feet in height. The top of the box (landing surface) should measure a minimum of 18 to 24 inches. Any less of a landing area would be dangerous. Because of the popularity of plyometrics in recent years, specialized, adjustable plyometric boxes have been developed and are available through most sporting goods outlets and fitness catalogs.

- *Medicine balls*: Medicine balls are used in a variety of conditioning disciplines, some of which have been previously discussed in this book. For plyometric training purposes, they are used for executing different throws and jumps.

- *Weighted vests*: The weighted vest is an outstanding tool for increasing explosiveness. Many athletes in jump-oriented sports such as volleyball and basketball routinely make use of this equipment in their plyometric training. Because the resistance is evenly distributed throughout the upper torso, plyometric drills performed with a weighted vest are relatively safe.

- *Ankle weights and strength shoes*: As a rule, it is discouraged to use any weighted equipment below the knee during plyometric training. Ankle weights and strength shoes fit into this category. Wearing these products and ones like them while engaging in intense jumping or movement training can contribute to aggravating the patella tendon in the front of the knee. This condition can keep you out of action for extended periods of time.

Training Surface

All plyometric training should be executed on soft surfaces. Rubberized running tracks, specialized plyometric training pads, and low-cut grass are best. Wood flooring is acceptable, albeit somewhat harder on the joints. Engaging in plyometric on hard surfaces, such as pavement or on uneven terrain, should be avoided.

Footwear

Because the large majority of plyometric exercises are of the high-impact variety, it is essential that you wear the proper footwear during your training sessions. Basketball or cross-training sneakers are suggested for plyometric workouts. This type of footwear provides lateral support, is sufficiently cushioned, and has non-slip soles. Running or jogging shoes lack lateral stability and leave you susceptible to twisted knees and ankles, thus they should not be used for plyometrics. Unless working out in the sand, engaging in plyometrics barefoot is also not recommended.

Schedule Description

Program Length

The length of a softball player's plyometric program will depend on a host of variables including the dynamics of your season, strength and conditioning level, and athletic ability. Most explosive sport athletes (football players, basketball players, volleyball players, etc.) only engage in plyometric training during the off-season, usually for 12 to 16 weeks in the mid to late off-season after they've developed the requisite strength and conditioning. Because participating in their respective sports entails constant explosive movements, additional plyometric workouts during the competitive season would cause overtraining in short order.

Softball players, on the other hand, can incorporate plyometric workouts on a semi-year round basis, as their sport does not encompass the physical demands of the aforementioned activities. Therefore, most softball plyometric programs will last from approximately the mid off-season right on through the regular campaign. As discussed throughout this section, plyometrics is a very demanding form of training, so implementing it carefully is suggested.

Workouts Per Week

Plyometric workouts should take place no more than twice per week. The individual sessions will be separated by a minimum of 48 to 72 hours.

Sets and Repetitions

As with strength training, sets and repetitions will vary with an athlete's needs, level of strength and fitness, experience with plyometrics, and time of year. Typically, a total of 100 to 200 contacts (repetitions) per workout should occur. For best results, spread the repetitions among three to four different plyometric drills. Three to six sets per exercise are recommended. The repetition range will be 8 to 15.

Rest between Sets

The level of intensity at which you are training will determine the rest periods between sets of plyometric exercises. For warm-up and low-intensity sets, one-minute rest intervals should be sufficient. High-intensity efforts will require up to three minutes of rest before beginning another set. Once you've become familiar with your own personal ability and level of conditioning, planning rest periods for plyometric training will become clear.

Workout Duration

Most plyometric workouts will range between 20 to 40 minutes. Again, much depends on your level of strength, conditioning, and experience with the training discipline. Regardless of how well conditioned you are, engaging in plyometric sessions of over 40 minutes is not recommended.

Keys to Safe and Productive Plyometric Training

Preparation

Proper preparation is without question the most important factor to successful, injury-free plyometric training. Engaging in these demanding workouts without a solid strength and conditioning base is a recipe for failure, not to mention frustration and injury.

Athletes must have a minimum of 10 to 12 weeks of weight-room strength training behind them prior to embarking on a plyometric program. Lower-body strength work is most important, as jumping and landing are key components of plyometric training. Conventional guidelines suggest that athletes should be able to leg press 2.5 times their body weight and/or squat 1.5 times their body weight before commencing with intense plyometric workouts. These guidelines are just averages, and attaining the strength-to-body-weight ratios is not a prerequisite for all. But, it is still important to achieve a reasonably high degree of strength, conditioning, and flexibility before starting your plyometric training program.

Learn Proper Execution

Performing plyometric drills correctly is essential to safe and effective workouts. The high-impact nature of plyometrics requires you to pay close attention to execution or risk injury. For best results, perform your first few training sessions at half speed, focusing on technique and form, rather than velocity and intensity. It is also advisable to seek out an experienced sports training specialist to help guide you through your beginning plyometric workouts.

Warm-Up and Cool-Down

Plyometric training, similar to all conditioning disciplines, requires a full warm-up and cool-down. Refer to Chapter 1 for a detailed explanation of warm-up and cool-down techniques.

Progression

Once proper technique is mastered, you should aspire to progress from the simpler plyometric movements to the more advanced variety. Intensity should be ramped up as well. As with strength training, progression is the name of the game here.

Effort and Intensity

Plyometric drills are designed to be performed at a high level of intensity. Once your warm-up sets are concluded, it is essential that every movement in your workout be executed with all-out effort.

Be Creative

While the drills detailed at the conclusion of this chapter are a good start, they provide only a small sampling of the many plyometric exercises available to you. Virtually hundreds of plyometric drills exist to be used. Once you master the basics, feel free to experiment with a variety of plyometric exercises. It is even suggested that you design your own movements and use them in your program. This creative approach will make your workouts more interesting and ultimately more successful.

Who Should Not Engage in Plyometrics

Plyometric exercise is recommended for most improvement-conscious softball players. However, some individuals should avoid this type of training. The following three scenarios illustrate instances where athletes should not engage in plyometric:

- *Pre-adolescents*: Pre-adolescent athletes, regardless of their physical maturity, should refrain from using plyometrics as a training tool. The risk of injury to muscles, bones, and joints is substantially higher prior to puberty than it is afterward. Youngsters are better served using their time and energy perfecting softball skills and improving their general conditioning than they are pushing the improvement envelope experimenting with advanced, high-impact training methods such as plyometrics.

- *Injured athletes*: This should be obvious, but all injured athletes or athletes with a history of lower-body ailments should abstain from using plyometrics. Even after you've rehabilitated successfully from an injury, it is best to use caution with this type of high-impact training. Remember, plyometrics and injuries don't mix, unless, of course, your goal is to worsen your injured condition.

- *Large athletes*: Large athletes must take great care with plyometrics. Some may opt to skip the training discipline altogether. The force of most landings during plyometric drills is high, and larger softball players are much more susceptible to impact related injury than their smaller counterparts. If, as a bigger athlete, you decide to incorporate plyometrics into your training, you may reduce your risk of injury by choosing simpler exercises, such as rim touches, double leg jumps, or cone hops.

Don't Overdo It

Just to re-emphasize, plyometrics, while performance enhancing, is an extremely demanding form of athletic conditioning. Too much plyometric work can cause overtraining and body breakdown for even the most gifted of athletes. Work hard during your plyometric sessions; just keep things in perspective and try not to overdo it. By approaching your plyometric training in this manner you will not be disappointed (or injured).

Beginner Plyometric Drills

Drill: Rim Touches

Execution: Facing a basketball rim or other elevated object such as a football goal post, assume an erect and balanced stance, with your head up and eyes fixed on the rim. Proceed by bending quickly to the jumping position (approximately three-quarters to parallel) an instantaneously explode upward toward the target, reaching up with one hand as high as possible. Repeat for the required repetitions, always focusing on popping up off the floor quickly.

Drill: Double-Leg Tuck Jumps

Execution: Assume an erect and balanced stance with your head straight and your eyes focused in front off you. Continue by bending quickly into the jumping position and immediately spring straight up as high as possible, while concurrently pulling your knees up toward your chest. During the jump phase of the drill, your arms should be positioned straight out in front of you. Similar to rim touches, the idea is to pop off the floor quickly upon landing.

Drill: Front Cone/Barrier Hops

Execution: Place a small cone or barrier (approximately 6 to 12 inches in height) directly in front of you. With your feet shoulder-width apart and your knees flexed, broad jump over the cone/barrier, concentrating on jumping as high as possible. During the airborne phase of the drill your body should be in a straight line. After your landing, turn 180 degrees and repeat the jump. Continue for the required number of repetitions.

Drill: Overhead Medicine Ball Toss

Execution: Stand with your knees slightly flexed and your feet close together, holding an appropriately weighted medicine ball overhead. Step forward explosively and release the ball when it reaches head height. Try to throw the ball as far as you can. Repeat for the required number of repetitions.

Intermediate Plyometric Drills

Drill: Lateral Cone/Barrier Jumps

Execution: Place a cone or barrier (6 to 18 inches in height depending on your athletic ability) on the ground. Stand sideways to the cone/barrier with your knees flexed and your feet at shoulder width. Proceed to jump laterally back and forth over the cone for the required number of repetitions.

Drill: Power Skips

Execution: Starting in a slow jog, gradually pick up speed, exaggerating your arm swing and knee lift. Your upper leg of the driving knee should be slightly above parallel to the running surface. Attempt to cover as much distance as possible during the airborne phase of the drill. As with all plyometric running and jumping exercises, try to spend as little time as possible in contact with the ground.

Drill: Backward Medicine Ball Toss

Execution: Stand with your knees bent and your feet slightly wider than shoulder width and pick up an appropriately weighted medicine ball from the ground. Proceed to swing the ball between your legs and, as your forearms come just short of your thighs, reverse course and throw the ball powerfully up over your head as far as possible. Repeat for the required number of repetitions.

Drill: Plyometric Push-Ups

Execution: With your feet raised behind you on a box or a step, assume a conventional push-up position. The box/step should range between six and 12 inches depending on your size and strength. Begin by pushing up explosively, allowing your hands to leave the ground. When your hands return to the ground, catch yourself and immediately explode upward for another repetition. Repeat for the required number of repetitions.

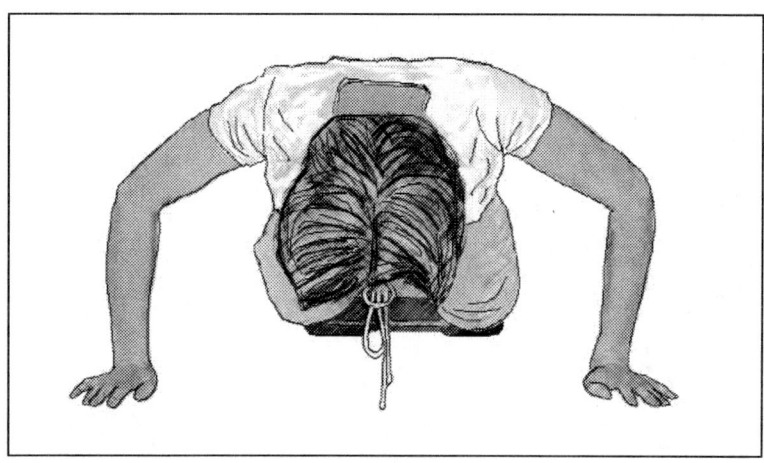

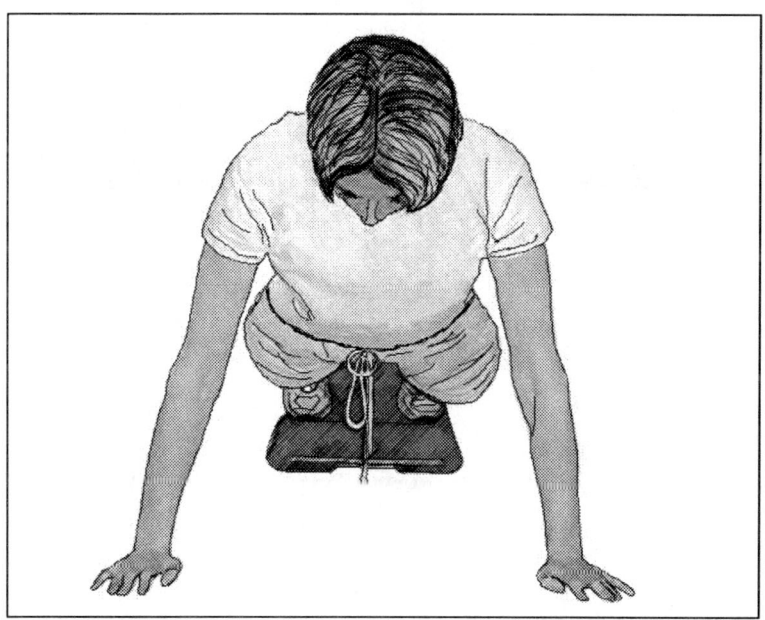

Advanced Plyometric Drills

Drill: Lateral Box Jumps

Execution: Stand sideways to a box with your knees comfortably flexed and your feet at shoulder width. The box will vary in height between one to three feet, depending on your athletic ability. Proceed to jump laterally up on to the box, landing under control on two feet. Hop down and immediately explode back up. Repeat for the required number of repetitions. Alternating sides each set.

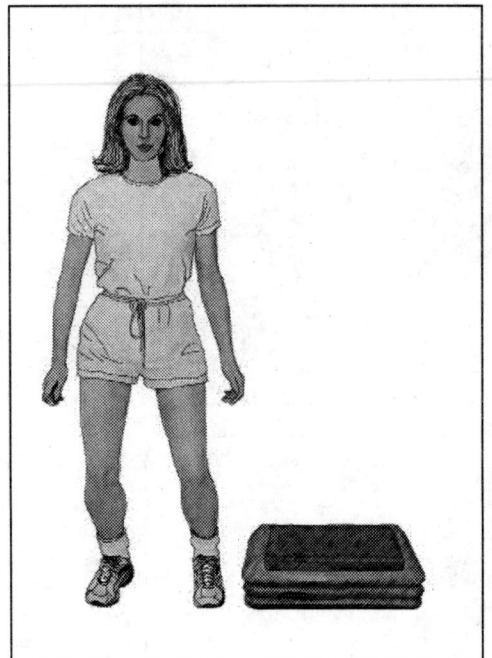 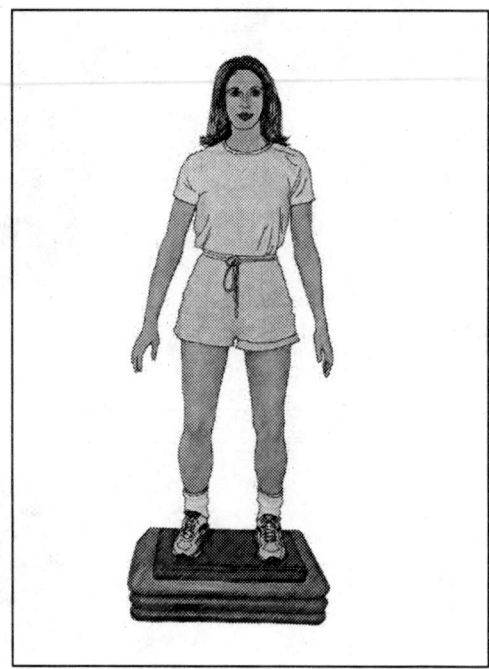

Drill: Front Box Jumps with Step Down

Execution: Stand facing a box, with your knees flexed, feet shoulder-width apart, and hands at your sides. The height of the box will vary from one to three feet, depending on your athletic ability. Jump on to the box, landing under control on two feet. Pause briefly, then step off the box with one foot, drop to the floor, and immediately spring as high as possible into the air (one repetition). Repeat for the required number of repetitions.

Drill: Medicine Ball Squat Jump

Execution: Begin by assuming a shoulder-width stance, with your feet pointed slightly outward. Take hold of an appropriately weighted medicine ball and place it comfortably behind your neck. Proceed to squat down until your upper legs are approximately parallel to the floor and explode upward. Throughout the drill, keep the resistance (medicine ball) in contact with your neck and shoulders. Repeat for the required number of repetitions.

Drill: Multiple Front Box Jumps

Execution: Line up three to five one-foot high boxes, spaced three to five feet apart. Face the line of boxes in the jumping position (knees flexed, feet at shoulder width, and hands at your sides.) Proceed to jump on and off each box in succession until the end of the row. Deliberately walk back to the front of the line and repeat for the required number of repetitions.

15

Cross Training Options for Softball Players

While the exercise choices in *Peak Conditioning Training for Softball* are certainly sufficient to keep even the most advanced softball player in top-flight condition, this book wouldn't be complete without some cross training options. Cross training periodically has many advantages. It helps to prevent overuse injuries, assists in heading off fitness plateaus, and, perhaps most beneficial, keeps your workouts from growing stale. This chapter reviews seven different training modalities softball players may want to consider incorporating into their year-round conditioning program.

Play Other Sports

Participating in other sports either recreationally or competitively during the off-season is highly recommended for softball players. Some of the best include field hockey, lacrosse, basketball, volleyball, soccer, and track and field. All the mentioned activities require explosive and agile movements, functional strength, precise footwork, and a high level of physical conditioning—certainly all attributes that can be translated onto the softball field.

Engaging in other sports during your softball downtime provides psychological benefits as well. It gives you a total mental break from the game, as your full attention is focused on another athletic activity. This break will help you to recharge your batteries and build up excitement and intensity for the upcoming softball season.

While partaking in different sports during your off-season months is encouraged, it is important that softball training and improvement remain the priority. All other endeavors should supplement your softball workouts and not the other way around.

Jumping Rope

Every softball player should own a jump rope. In fact, every softball player should own three jump ropes: a light-handled, easy-turning rope; a heavy-handled rope; and a heavy-corded rope. Training regularly with a variety of jump ropes will help you improve many aspects of your softball conditioning and athleticism. Working out with an easy-turning rope will enhance your footwork, hand speed, quickness, and coordination. It is also a great tool for improving your aerobic conditioning, as the rope's easy-turning feature will allow you to jump for extended periods of time.

Jumping with the heavy-handled variety will strengthen your hands, fingers, and forearms to a large degree, which will improve your ability to swing and throw with power and authority. Training with this type of rope can also provide you with a terrific lactic acid system workout.

Exercising with a heavy-corded rope is great for conditioning your ATP-PC system and will aid in building strength throughout your upper body, especially the all-important shoulder region. Young softball players should first spend some time training with the light-handled and heavy-handled ropes before moving on to heavy-corded rope workouts.

Jumping rope is highly recommended for all softball players, but the benefits are especially pertinent for young athletes, who are just coming to terms athletically with their ever growing bodies. Training with a jump rope will help youngsters get their upper and lower bodies in sync, allowing them to develop body awareness and overall coordination.

Tips for Effective Jump Rope Workouts

- *Rope length*: A jump rope should be long enough to reach armpit to armpit, while passing under both feet. If you have trouble procuring a proper-sized rope, jump rope manufactures will be happy to custom design one for you. Jump rope manufactures are listed in most fitness product catalogs.

- *Turning the rope*: Turning a jump rope is a fairly simple process. It entails turning your hands and wrists in a natural forward circle. Your upper arms should be held close to your torso, and your forearms should be pointed downward at a 45-degree angle. Your wrists and hands do most of the work when turning a light-handled rope; your forearms come more prominently into play when turning a heavy-handled rope; and your shoulder girdle is highly engaged when turning a heavy-cored rope.

- *Where to jump*: It is best to conduct your rope-jumping workouts on semi-soft surfaces. Some of the best include rubberized running tracks, artificial turf, or specialized rope-jumping pads. Hard surfaces such as concrete, asphalt, or blacktop should be avoided when jumping rope.

- *Warm-up lower legs thoroughly*: Jumping rope regularly can be extremely taxing on the lower legs (calves, shins, and ankles). Therefore, it is imperative that you warm-up and stretch your lower legs fully prior to each and every rope-jumping session.

- *Jumping patterns*: Although you have virtually hundreds of jumping patterns at your disposal when jumping rope, the following three basic methods are all you need to enjoy productive workouts:

  ✓ *Alternate foot jump*: The athlete jumps once each rope turn, alternating between her left foot and right foot. Jumping in this manner resembles running in place.

  ✓ *Two-foot jump*: The athlete jumps once each rope turn, with both feet hitting the ground simultaneously. Your feet should be slightly closer than shoulder width when executing this jumping pattern.

  ✓ *Skip jump*: The athlete jumps once each rope turn, alternating landings in no set sequence between left foot, right foot, and both feet simultaneously.

Once you master these basic jump rope techniques, feel free to learn and experiment with more complicated jumping patterns as you see fit.

Stadium Step Running

Athletes in a variety of sports incorporate stadium step running in their conditioning programs. All you need to do is locate a reasonably large stadium (most colleges with a football team have them) and go to it.

The emphasis when running stadium steps should be on high knee lift. You want to explode upward from step to step, spending as little time on each stair as possible. It is always important to maintain body balance as you ascend. Because your legs will be fatigued once you reach the top of the stairs, it is imperative that you are extremely careful on your descent so as to avoid stumbling. By coming down the stairs mindfully, you will avoid any mishaps.

For softball players, stadium step workouts will be used periodically as a supplement to your resistance sprinting routine, usually in lieu of uphill running. Athletes with a history of knee problems should avoid this cross training option.

Spinning

Spinning is an intense form of interval training performed on specially designed stationary bikes. It is one of the few fitness club creations that has survived the test of time. (Many fitness industry classes are faddish in nature.) The reason spinning has endured is simple. It provides a tremendous low-impact interval workout that is easy to follow and readily available in most communities.

The key to a productive spinning class begins and ends with the instructor. An experienced, enthusiastic spinning teacher can take you through a fantastic workout, one that will contribute greatly to your overall conditioning. On the other hand, training under a below par class leader is nothing but a waste of time. The good news on this front is, because of spinning's longevity and continued popularity, numerous qualified instructors exist throughout the United States as well as worldwide.

Softball players are best served incorporating spinning workouts in phase two of their conditioning programs when lactic acid system training is the priority. These workouts can also be used periodically in-season during phase four (maintenance phase).

Boxing Training

Boxing training has become an extremely popular form of exercise for athletes in many sports including softball. It involves a combination of shadow boxing, footwork drills, rope skipping, abdominal training, medicine ball work, hitting heavy and speed bags, and ring work with a trainer. Live sparring is neither necessary nor recommended for softball players.

The benefits of regular boxing workouts are many. They include strengthening and loosening the muscles of the upper body, improving footwork and hand-eye coordination, and shaping up the all-important core of the body. A boxing session also provides both aerobic and anaerobic conditioning benefits.

Although many commercial health clubs and fitness centers feature boxing classes, it is highly recommended that you search out a traditional boxing gym for your lessons and workouts. These gyms not only possess the proper equipment but provide you with experienced trainers, most of whom have fought competitively in the squared circle for many years. Table 15-1 presents a sample boxing workout.

1 round shadow boxing (warm-up)	2 rounds in-ring footwork drills
1 round rope skipping	2 rounds rope skipping
3 rounds heavy bag work	2 rounds abdominal training
2 rounds speed bag work	1 round shadow boxing (cool-down)

- ▸ The workout is based on three-minute rounds and one-minute rest intervals between rounds.
- ▸ Total workout time = 57 minutes

Table 15-1. A sample boxing workout

Sand Workouts

Exercising on sand is a fantastic way to mix up your movement training (plyometrics, quickness/agility, balance, and speed), while at the same time cultivating significant fitness, strength, and athleticism benefits. Sand workouts are also outstanding for lower body injury rehabilitation. Soft sand gives substantially on each footfall, thus making it easy on the joints and the body in general.

If you don't have the luxury of living near a beach, check your local colleges and high schools, as many now feature man-made sand pits designed for training. Otherwise, a simple sand box, sand volleyball court, or long jump pit will do.

Footwear is optional for sand workouts. Many trainers prefer to go barefoot. While others opt for wearing some type of basketball, cross training, or running shoes. Do what's most comfortable for you. Before beginning each sand workout check the terrain carefully for sharp objects, such as broken glass or cracked sea shells. Additionally, try to find a stretch of beach/sand that is relatively even for your sand workouts.

Circuit Training

Circuit training consists of a variety of exercises performed one after the other with very little rest between sets. A typical circuit involves 8 to 12 exercises or stations and can be ran through anywhere from one to four times depending upon your individual conditioning level.

Originally circuit training pertained almost exclusively to strength training, as Nautilus equipment and its inherent training system became popular throughout the fitness world in the mid-1970s. Today, however, creative conditioning specialists routinely devise circuits that incorporate many different training modalities. As you become more experienced with your strength and conditioning training, feel free to come up with your own circuits that fit your personal needs. Table 15-2 details a circuit workout you may want to try.

Jump rope = 60 seconds

Crunches = 25 reps

Push-ups = 20 reps

Medicine ball side tosses = 15 each side

Body weight squats = 20 reps

Lateral line hops = 30 seconds

Medicine ball push presses = 15 reps

Wall slides = hold for 60 seconds

Table 15.2. Sample circuit training workout

About the Author

Tom Emma is the president of Power Performance, Inc., a company that specializes in training athletes in strength, conditioning, and athletic enhancement techniques. He is a graduate of Duke University, where he was a three-year starter on the basketball team and squad captain his senior year. He was drafted by the Chicago Bulls in the 1983 NBA draft. Tom has a masters degree from Columbia University and lives in New York City. He is the author of five books, including *Peak Conditioning Training for Basketball* and *Peak Conditioning Training for Volleyball*, both of which were published by Coaches Choice.